GW01019283

SMALL ANTIQUES FOR THE COLLECTOR

SMALL ANTIQUES

FOR THE COLLECTOR

by

D. C. Gohm

Arco Publishing Company, Inc.

New York

A[1]

Published by ARCO PUBLISHING COMPANY, INC., 219 Park Avenue South,
New York, NY, 10003
Copyright © John Gifford Ltd. 1968
Library of Congress Catalog Number 71-11642
ISBN 0 668 02266 3
Printed in Great Britain by The Hillingdon Press (Westminster Press Ltd) Uxbridge, Middlesex

CONTENTS

LIST OF ILLUSTRATIONS

BLACK AND WHITE PLATES

COLOUR PLATES

INTRODUCTION

The objective of this book is to introduce the new, and potentially new collector to small antiques, and having made the introduction, to lend a guiding hand during the early, maybe confusing days, until he is able to make his way on his own initiative.

It is not intended that this book should be a reference work, the subject of antiques is too enormous, and would require too much detailed, perhaps even boring, descriptive text, to be contained successfully in one volume. It could tend also to take away some of the pleasure of studying antiques to someone unaccustomed to the subject. Such works are for later study.

Antiques cover every type of object made prior to the last 100 years or so. (Antique furniture is usually required to have been made prior to 1830.) Their numbers are legion, and their prices vary from a few shillings to vast sums so high, that no real price can be established. Such articles are, in fact, " priceless ".

Prices of antiques vary, depending upon variety, current collecting fashions, and supply and condition. Therefore, except in a very few instances, no attempt has been made to quote current prices, which could well be incorrect by the time this book goes to press.

COLLECTING

Collecting is a very personal matter, therefore the choice of subject must be left to the individual. Silver for instance, may send you in raptures, or it may leave you stone cold. On the other hand, a casual introduction to some small item could be the first step that would lead eventually to a life-long, all consuming, interest in this particular subject.

There are, of course, many ways to form a collection, but for the average collector of average means it is better to decide either to specialise in one field, or to furnish your home with a miscellany of antiques covering a wide range of subjects.

Specialization offers the best all round advantages, because the knowledge required is more concentrated, and the field can be widened or narrowed to suit means and inclination. For instance, silver is a wide specialist subject, but it can be narrowed by collecting any particular series of items such as snuff boxes, pill boxes, vinaigrettes, or simply any small silver box.

Having decided to collect in a particular field, the next step will be to gain some knowledge of the subject, before parting with any cash. The text of this book should be read carefully under the appropriate heading, but remember that written knowledge is a great aid, but it must be used in conjunction with practical experience. Whenever possible visit museums, auction rooms, antique dealers, and junk markets. Handle the specimens, examine them in detail to confirm your theoretical knowledge, and get to know the " feel " of your subject.

Antique dealers of repute will not try to " catch you ", they are much too jealous of their reputation, but they will often spend quite a lot of their time talking to you if they are not too busy, and they find you are genuinely interested.

Do not expect to pick up valuable pieces for next to nothing. You may well, now and again, buy very com-

7

petitively, but the days when rare items can be bought from markets and junk shops for shillings is over. It *can* still happen, of course, but such good luck is usually the result of the buyer having considerably more knowledge and experience than the vendor.

This does not mean that mini-bargains are impossible, if you know your subject well, you will often find pieces under market value.

Search around the odd corners of antique and junk shops for really interesting new items, it's laborious, often very exasperating, yet offers unexpected rewards for those collectors with the necessary perseverance.

Silver collecting is relatively easy, the hall-mark will tell you quite a lot about the quality and origin, but other subjects are not so specific. Furniture is a more difficult problem, quite modern pieces are produced in antique styles, some are very obvious and sold as reproductions but favoured designers have been imitated well out of their original period. This is where one has to become a detective, with a background knowledge of dates, techniques used, shapes and designs in vogue, and materials available at a given period, but although dates, materials, and facts available may well indicate that a piece is genuine, it could still be a skilful fake. In the final analysis, it will become a matter of experience. Remember that the general periods are not hard and fast demarcations, trends in fashions and design were certainly different within the reigns, depending upon the various influences, but an overlap was inevitable in what was, in fact, a continual evolutionary process.

Pottery and Porcelain are not two words for the same thing. In general terms pottery is made from an opaque, coarse clay, and remains opaque after firing. Porcelain on the other hand is finer and generally translucent after firing. Like all successful new products, both pottery and porcelain makers with original ideas, have had their imitators. Direct forgeries will often require the knowledge of an expert to detect them. Modern methods of investigation, including laboratory testing, may well be necessary to establish authenticity of the most skilful fakes.

It must now be quite obvious to the new collector that no specific instructions or rules can be laid down to guarantee every stage in the acquisition of small antiques. Wherever possible, however, important factors and suggestions have been included under the appropriate headings. This, it is hoped, will increase the pleasure, that can be obtained in the fascinating search for antiques.

BOOKS

Whatever your interest, there is certain to have been a book written about it. Books have been published to cover every conceivable subject. They are found in a variety of sizes, either profusely illustrated or with little, or no illustrations at all.

The attraction of old books may be the visual appeal of fine bindings, and interesting illustrations. They also interest by their content of information, and by their connection with the past. Many collectors are swayed more by the sheer beauty of the binding than by the book itself and rarely read the contents. No matter from what your personal interest in books may stem, it is certain that a worthwhile collection can be built up.

There is a fantastic wide range of books and consequently there is a wide range of prices. When compared with other forms of collecting it will be found that the pursuit of old books *can* be undertaken with moderate means, if you adjust your taste to your pocket.

Browsing around old bookshops is almost a national pastime, every English town of any size has an antiquarian book shop, which will supply catalogues if requested to do so. Old books can even be found on the stalls in market places, and tucked away in the corners of junk-shops.

Really fine English antique bookbindings are expensive, and will be reserved for the man with a large banking account, therefore we must specialise in our early collecting days with something less elaborate, such as early 19th century signed bindings, or the plainer trade bindings. Having chosen the field in which it is intended to specialise the next consideration will be condition, this is an important aspect so do not accept books that have been extensively restored, or are in a very bad state. It is much better to have a few books of good quality than a book shelf full of soiled and ragged specimens. It must be remembered however, that the leathers used in England, with the exception of the best morocco, did not last well, therefore it may be necessary to make some compromise in this respect.

The binding leathers will give an indication of date, mediaeval manuscripts commonly used deer skin, or sheep skin which was either pink or white.

During the 16th century, the majority of books with decorative bindings were covered with calf, irrespective of whether they were blocked in blind, or tooled.

From about 1525 onwards a soft vellum became popular for the smaller undecorated books. The first half of the 17th century gave us morocco, usually in brown or olive green (morocco is tanned goats skin). From about 1650 blue and red moroccos first appeared, and it became the normal material for the finest bindings of the Restoration period. Gold tooled vellum bindings were also fashionable during the early 17th century but the material gradually fell into disuse on the plainer bindings in favour of sheep or calf. During the 18th century sheep was used for the more common or cheaper works. From about 1770 we find the early forms of book cloth which was, in fact, a type of canvas. It is interesting to note that the early paper covered boards cf books was intended as a temporary protection until properly bound.

An English technique originating in the 17th century and revived about 1785 by Edwards of Halifax, known as fore-edge painting, now provides a rather unusual facet of book collecting. Fore-edge painting was, literally painting the fore-edge of every page, so that when they were fanned out and held, the decoration appeared as painted views, or conversation pieces. When the book was in its normal closed position the edges of the paper were gilded in the normal way, and the painting concealed and protected. Just fan out the edges again and the pictures will reappear. Good specimens of fore-edge painting will command very high prices and it will often be found that the literary contents of the book is unimportant.

There are many fine 18th and 19th century books on travel and topography, these usually have very fine engravings, but unfortunately such is the popularity of prints, that many print dealers are seeking these books for breaking. The prints are removed, coloured, and sold individually.

Book dealers who issue catalogues invariably show the size of the book. It might not be out of place to include here a few words on book sizes.

The book pages are made by printing on a large sheet of paper which is subsequently folded, therefore the size of the book depends upon the size of the sheet, and the way the sheets are folded. Detailed below are most of the sizes that were in common use, these of course were sub-divided into large and small.

Foolscap	$13\frac{1}{2}$	x	17 inches.
Post	15	x	19 inches.
Crown	15	x	20 inches.
Demy	$17\frac{1}{2}$	x	$22\frac{1}{2}$ inches.
Medium	18	x	23 inches.
Royal	20	x	25 inches.
Imperial	22	x	30 inches.

When the sheet of paper is folded only once, this is known as folio, it does in fact make four pages; if the sheet was folded once again, i.e. folded twice, it would now provide four leaves or eight pages; this is known as quarto; folded once again into eight leaves, it provides 16 pages; this book would be known as octavo. It will now be obvious that a Crown Octavo is $7\frac{1}{2}''$ x $5''$ and a Royal Octavo is $10''$ x $6\frac{1}{4}''$. There are other formulas that decide the format of a book, which depends upon how its sheets are folded, and then how these sheets are gathered into quires, but at this stage it is not intended to describe book formats. The new collector will have quite enough to think about just learning book sizes.

General Care

Having obtained the nucleus of a new collection, it is as well to know how to look after it. Excessive dry heat will make both the paper and the leather brittle, so endeavour to put your books somewhere where they will not receive direct heat from fire or sun. Excessive dampness also is just as injurious, this can lead to the growth of moulds. Sulphurous atmosphere can cause the leather to decay, and do not forget insect pests. The leathers of books can be treated with a dressing specifically manufactured for this purpose. Some of the preparations manufactured for shoes, provide an excellent media for use on real leather, but do not use commercial saddle soap or any of the furniture polishes or creams. The conditions prevailing in a normal living room of a house will be ideal for keeping your book collection, this means we do not have to be too fussy, but it would be unwise to leave valuable books in a bedroom that was subject to a slightly damp atmosphere, or a room like an attic that is rarely used, otherwise we may provide ideal conditions for small insect life that likes to feed on the paste, or chew the paper.

GLOSSARY

Azured: A term derived from the method of indicating the colour azure in heraldic engraving, shown by a series of slanting, horizontal lines.

Beau livre: Books with original illustrations, in this sense, wood or copper engravings, lino cuts, and lithographs would be considered "Original" works, as the artist would have executed the plate. Illustrations produced by these techniques automatically set a limit to the numbers that could be produced due to plate wear.

Bevelled Edges: Descriptive of the edges of the boards, or covers, which have been angled before being covered.

Blind: A term used to describe decorations or lettering on the binding that has been impressed only, and is devoid of any colour, such as gold.

Block: A block made of wood or metal, without a handle, carrying a design for decorating the cover of a book, intended for use in a blocking press.

Boards: The hard cover of a book.

Calf: Leather made from the hide of a calf, commonly used in book binding.

Cartouche: A type of decorative label, sometimes very ornate with scroll outer framing, but also loosely describes any round, oval, or decorative label.

Colour-plate books: A broad description for books with colour plates, irrespective of the process used, i.e. printed in full colour, or aquatinted, engraved, or lithographed and subsequently coloured by hand.

Deckle Edge: The uncut edge of hand made paper, usually slightly wavy.

Endpapers: Double l e a v e s added at the front and back of a book, the outer leaf being stuck to the inner face of the cover. 16th and 17th century leather and vellum bound books were sometimes without end-papers.

Etruscan Style: From about 1780 to 1825 calf bindings were decorated with classical designs by the use of staining acids. This type of finish is termed Etruscan Style.

Foxing: Brown coloured spots disfiguring pages of a book, caused by damp and impurities in the paper.

Halfbound: This usually means the spine and outer corners of the cover only is leather covered. The rest of the covers finished in paper or cloth.

Levant: A type of morocco, loose grained, and held in high esteem for the past 100 years.

Limited Edition: An edition which is restricted to a definite number of copies.

Morocco: Originally used to describe leather made from the skin of North African goats, but now used to describe any goat skin leather.

Panel: Rectangular outlines, or panels, either in between the bands of the spine or on the sides of a book.
The outline can consist of a single line or a number of lines, blind, or gilt.

Re-backed: Renewal of the spine, or backstrip.

Re-cased: Fixing a book that has become loosely formed, more strongly between the covers.

Roll: A tool used to obtain a continuous or repetitive design.

Sheep: A soft, almost grain-free leather obtained from sheep.

Wrappers: Paper covers, either plain, marbled or printed. Equivalent to a modern paper-back.

BRASS

Man started using metal many centuries ago, well before any historical records were maintained. Old civilizations were familiar with tin, copper, bronze, and iron, and of course gold and silver.

Copper and tin were often found deposited quite near to each other, and it is probable that this proximity, originally combined them accidentally to provide the alloy bronze. Bronze has been in use from approximately 1000 B.C.! About this time, iron also was being smelted in Central Europe, and had certainly reached Britain well before the arrival of Julius Caesar sometime during 55 B.C.

The middle ages saw Germany developing the mining of copper and the subsequent manufacture of brass. Flanders was also one of the early users of brass which was employed to embellish churches with effigy brasses. At this time, Britain was using the alloys of copper to provide armour and implements of war.

Before we start collecting brass it is as well to understand the difference between brass and bronze, and so avoid any possible confusion. Antique bronze is generally accepted to be an alloy of copper and tin, and has a decided red hue. It is a very malleable material that lends itself to forming by hammering. Brass is an alloy of copper and zinc, or copper and calamine, and has a yellow hue. Its main advantage over bronze is that it can be cast satisfactorily, even in thin sections for the manufacture of furniture brasses.

The first brass to be manufactured in this country dates back to approximately the 16th century. Brass, however, was used in this country centuries before it was manufactured here. Early brass work was executed from material that had been imported from Germany and the Netherlands in flat sheets. This early imported material was mainly used by the church for church brasses, these are now eagerly sought by collectors interested in brass rubbings.

The first brass made in this country during the Elizabethan period was made of copper and calamine, but it was, in fact, more like a bronze than the brass we know today, which is a composition of copper and zinc.

Latten is an old word for brass, and refers specifically to brass sheets that have been made from ingots, and flattened by beating with a horse- or water-powered hammer, consequently latten can be recognised as a flat brass sheet which shows the marks of hammering.

It was during the reign of Queen Elizabeth I that the first patent was granted to William Humfrey and Christopher Schutz which gave them the monopoly of working in the new material brass. It was not until some time during the 18th century that the method of producing flat sheet by hammering was superseded by the more modern methods employed by the rolling mill, as it is still produced today.

Brass is an excellent craftsman's material, it has a good colour, and it is ductile and malleable. It can be joined easily, and polishes very readily, and has a relatively high resistance to the action of the atmosphere.

Many articles can be made from brass sheet, by cutting, hammering and forming. But such is the versatility of the material that it can be both cast and spun. The method of spinning is to secure a disc of brass between the tail-stock and the headstock of a lathe. The headstock will carry a pattern shaped to the desired form, this can be made of any hard wood or if a large quantity of spinnings are required, it can be made of metal. The disc is now rotated in the lathe and a tool pressed against the rotating surface forcing the disc to conform to the shape of the pattern. Articles that have been produced by spinning show concentric circles made by the pressure from the tool.

Castings are produced from a master pattern and the use of a special sand. The pattern is put into a box that is split in the middle, and the sand rammed tightly around it. The box is then opened to allow the pattern to be removed without disturbing the sand. When the two halves of the box have been put together again a cavity in the sand equal to the pattern will be left in the centre of the box, metal is then poured into this cavity. When cooled, the metal will be a solid replica of the master pattern.

Why not start your brass collection with horse brasses? These decorative pieces of horse furniture have been known in England for over 2000 years, but it was not until the 1840's that more than a single brass face piece was used.

Pieces earlier than 1850 are rare but from the 1860's they were available in a wide variety of designs. They were used hanging from the martingale, and on each side of the runners and the shoulders. There were forehead pieces, ear brasses for hanging behind the ears, and up to 20 pendant pieces.

Briefly the evolution of horse brasses based on manufacturing techniques is as follows.

1750 to 1800. Horse brasses from this period are very rare, they were chiefly made in the form of Georgian sun flashes, and made by hand from hard latten.

Until about 1860. Horse brasses up to about 1860 are also rare. They were made from early brass containing calamine. Because castings are more porous than hammered sheet they tend to polish less readily, and contain surface flaws caused by trapped gas bubbles during the casting process.

1800 to approx. 1850. These are not so rare, but will be difficult to find. Usually made from rolled calamine brass, and they were fairly soft and dull in appearance.

Between 1830 to 1860. These were cast in fine brass alloy using copper and zinc (much the same as present day brass). Also cast in a high quality brass alloy of the Pinchbeck variety, and often coloured a reddish gold, with burnished highlights. These are now extremely rare. A type of metal known as Emersons brass was also used during this period, this was a copper spelter metal which produced a smooth surfaced, brilliantly gold coloured brass. Whilst these are not so rare as the Pinchbeck variety, they are still very uncommon.

1860's to about 1900. During the earlier part of this period more commercial alloys were used. Castings were finished by file and pierced by drilling, then carefully finished and polished.

Later in this period the brasses were produced by relatively modern methods of stamping from sheet and these were made almost exclusively in Birmingham and Walsall. Early examples, lead filled, are now very rare.

Stamped brasses made from sheet by machine, were much cheaper to produce as they were made in fairly long runs and used less material.

The purpose of horse brasses is believed to have originated by the desire of their owners to ward off evil spirits. Our Ancestors certainly believed in witchcraft, sorcery, and the power of the evil eye, and it is true that the majority of the designs used incorporate a symbol, which was intended to bring good luck, secure a favourable glance from some ancient and benevolent god, or to offer protection to both the horse and driver from the evil eye. During the middle ages sorcery and witchcraft was an accepted practice, and the effects of such beliefs can be observed today by the number of people who are still superstitious.

Horse brasses as such are a comparatively modern piece of horse furniture. They certainly did not exist in pre-Victorian times, although lucky charms and amulets in one form or another may well have been used in the past. There is no real evidence to show that horse brasses were intended for any other purpose than to decorate a horse.

Since the horse brass became popular for interior decoration, and as a collectors item, modern fakes have been made in great numbers. Fakes are usually cast, and treated with acids to give them an older appearance. Genuine old brasses have a feel and well worn appearance that is not easily copied. It can however, be very difficult to distinguish between fake and genuine example, but this can be done when you have gained experience of the subject.

Whilst making no attempt to provide a fully comprehensive history of horse brass design, the following explanations may however prove of interest.

The Acorn

This is a lucky symbol associated with agriculture.

Anchor

The motif or symbol of Saint Nicholas, an anchor superimposed upon a sun disc was used as a trade mark of the Bull Brewery Company.

Barrel

This is an obvious symbol used by many brewery companies for their horse brasses.

Bell

Bells have a special significance, by implication they are noisy instruments to frighten off evil spirits. Bells also have religious connections.

Bear

A popular Lincolnshire design.

Chrysanthemum

A flower like brass probably based upon the early lucky world design.

Churn

Usually associated with dairy man's horses.

Clasped Hands

A classic piece of Victorian design that originated about the time of Victoria's jubilee, many associations with friendly societies, etc.

Interlacing Knots

The endless knot was originally a Buddhist emblem of security.

Crescent

This symbol is probably used more than any other, and was used either in its pure form or incorporated in many designs. The crescent shaped moon was a symbol of the moon goddess and was believed to have special powers of protection against evil spirits.

Railway Engine

These are interesting brasses sometimes showing a

railway engine on rails and sometimes without. These were made originally for Railway Company Horses.

Pair of Fish

Probably a religious symbol but it is also an old Buddhist emblem of good luck.

Fleur-de-Lis

A very old symbol of good luck depicting a stylised version of The Lotus of Iris. This emblem has become identified with the Royal House of France.

Saint George and the Dragon

The patron saint of England, it was no doubt used on horse brasses because Saint George was one of the patron saints of the horse.

Heart and Sun Rays

Reputed to have originated in Warwickshire.

Horse Shoe

A well known lucky motif. Often shown in a cluster of three.

Rose

The association of the Tudor Rose with England makes this an obvious decorative piece.

Shamrock

This is of course the emblem of Ireland and has its associations with good luck.

Stars

Horse brasses incorporating stars with eight points and five points or rays have been used for horse brasses, and have associations with old mystic cults.

Three Tuns

The Ancient Company of Vintners used the three tuns as their coat of arms, brewery horses often were decorated with brasses showing a tun or a barrel.

The brief descriptions of horse brass designs given above, cover only a few of the possibilities. Should you wish to know more of the origin and meaning of the various designs that have been used for horse furniture, these have been well covered in a useful little book by R. A. Brown, Secretary to the Hackney Horse Society,

and titled " Horse Brasses, Their History and Origin ";
this book has been published by R. A. Brown.

Brass candlesticks have been in existence from as early
as the 12th century, but they are now, of course, very rare
and they are unlikely to be found, other than in the
museums or as part of church regalias. Therefore we
must content ourselves with pieces from the 18th century
onwards.

During the period 1700 to 1725, they were made
octagonal and ballister in shape. From about 1725 to
1760 the ballister became vase shaped, with a shell base.
During the latter part of the century the base became
square and the general design more classical.

Old brass is difficult to date, there were no hall marks
to guide us, neither were many pieces marked in any way,
however, it is possible to get a rough idea of the date of
a candlestick by examination of the method of construction. Up to about the late 17th century, the stem and
socket were cast in one piece and the base was either
attached by means of a screwed thread, or by a burred-
over projection. The projecting tongue was passed
through a hole in the centre of the base, and then
hammered or burred over to form a head which held it
securely in place, in much the same way as rivets hold
plates together today.

A new method of casting was introduced about 1670,
instead of the very solid, heavy castings used up to that
date, the new method allowed both the socket and stem
to be cast as separate pieces, which were subsequently
brazed together. The main advantage of this method
was of course the obvious saving in material.

Nineteenth century candlesticks were more or less
solid, one piece castings.

As previously stated, it is often very difficult to distinguish between genuine old brass and fairly modern
examples, but we can get a reasonable indication if we
look under the base of our candlesticks, or any other
hollow cast object and look at the surface. Most old brass
will have concentric rings made by a turning tool; if the

base has a rough impression formed by the sand during the casting process, it can be taken that the article is a modern production.

Brass foundries have existed in Britain since about the middle of the 18th century, there were certainly foundries in Birmingham at this time, producing a great variety of articles, some of which were very elegant and well worth collecting, others not so elegant and somewhat crudely made. However, the collector need not be dismayed, there is certain to be something he likes, such as old brass oil lamps, fenders, footwarmers, coalhods, braziers, funnels, furniture mounts, locks, skillets, not forgetting the wide range of nautical equipment and scientific instruments.

Cleaning and Care

There are many excellent proprietary polishes available providing they are used with reasonable care. Badly discoloured brass should be washed first in an ammonia solution to remove any surface dirt or grime. Then if you wish you can make up a solution with vinegar and common salt which will brighten the brass. Thoroughly wash and polish with a soft cloth afterwards. Furniture mounts, and handles on drawers, are best removed before cleaning, otherwise there is risk of spoiling the surrounding woodwork, and of filling the interstices with polish residue or bits of cloth. If however they are not readily removable the proprietary product Dura-glit can be used with care.

BYGONES

A bygone is a special kind of antique. All antiques are to some extent bygones but a general description would define a bygone as a functional item that had been replaced by a more advanced or by a better item for doing the same job.

Bygones are interesting in themselves, but the true collector will not be satisfied in just possessing the article. He will want to know its past history, the function, how

Back row, left to right: 19th century steak beater; 19th century mincing machine; 19th century, boxwood potato masher, made *en suite* with the piecrust roller in front—these were made in pairs as wedding gifts; late 18th century standing spice box, with radiating compartments. In front, left to right, strainer spoon; 17th or early 18th century lemon squeezer, and late 18th century or early 19th, boxwood, urn type lemon squeezer.
All English. *Formerly in the Collection of the late Rev. C. J. Sharp.*
(*In the Pinto Collection of Wooden Bygones, Birmingham Museum and Art Gallery*)

it worked, what it did, and if possible from where it came.

The 20th century is the age of automation and very sophisticated methods of doing things. Old crafts have

Back row, left to right: An early wine biber; an 18th century standing goblet; a tumbler stand, with immature coconut tumbler in it; a 16th century loving cup. Middle row: A selection of goblets of various shapes and sizes. Bottom row, left to right: Rare 18th century, lignum vitae tankard; beaker with simulated bands; burr maple beaker on ball feet and two more goblets. All English, with the exception of the burr maple beaker, which may be Swedish.

(*In the Pinto Collection of Wooden Bygones, Birmingham Museum and Art Gallery*)

been superseded by elegant modern machines that produce accurately and in vast numbers, consequently the
old craftsman's tools have fallen into disuse, and are
slowly but surely disappearing. Old methods of farming
have been superseded by mechanical aids, tractors now
carry the milk churns from the cow shed to the disposal
point, the milkman no longer delivers milk in cans, and
many of the old farming implements lie rotting in barns
or fields. Although there are still wheel-wrights, saddlers,
thatchers and coach builders, they are, no doubt, avail-
ing themselves of the benefits of progress, their old tools
dusty and rusty in some forgotten corner.

The following suggestions for collectors are not
categoric, but reflect the author's own ideas of what
should constitute a bygone.

Back row: Traditional cheese moulds, with weep holes in the base.
Front, left to right: Coopered piggin; crown, three dimensional butter
mould, formerly used at St. James's Palace, and a selection of butter
prints, three of the ejector type. All English. (*In the Pinto Collection
of Wooden Bygones. Birmingham Museum & Art Gallery.*)

Tools

There are a great number of tools that have become obsolete, and very soon will become expensive and difficult to find. Old craftsmen's tools of the Carpenter, Saddler, Thatcher, Cobbler and old farm implements are required by museums and collector alike. Not only are these articles required for their interest, but they are being used extensively as interior decorative pieces.

There is one disadvantage of collecting these items, one can hardly display an old plough in the dining room, but the variety is sufficiently large to permit items to be selected that can be contained within the normal house.

Household

These are usually small items and can be, and are, used as decorative pieces in old cottages, public houses, and even in new hotels.

Hand made door hinges, locks, footscrapers, caldrons, spits, grid-irons and scullery pieces, not forgetting old mouse traps, could be assembled under this heading.

Spinning Wheels

Spinning wheels have almost become a modern furnishing piece, especially if you are fortunate enough to own a period house or very old cottage. But do not be fooled by modern reproductions, the old ones were made to do a job of work, not for ornamental purposes only. Utility spinning wheels designed for cottages and crofters were practical machines and were made of hard wood and without much ornamentation, but those made for use in the drawing room of the elite, were more elegant affairs in walnut, ebony, or oak and inlaid with mother-of-pearl.

Tinder Boxes

A tinder box is a container for holding tinder, which is a material that ignites easily; a steel striker, and a piece of flint. The steel and flint are struck together to give a spark which causes the tinder to smoulder and with much huffing and puffing to burst into flames, that is if you are lucky.

Tinder boxes were made in wood, sometimes beautifully carved; in tin, with the means of holding a candle, and of various designs in brass, copper and plate.

A development of the tinder box was the " strike a light ", or tinder pistol. This resembled a pistol in shape, complete with stock. When triggered the hammer fell causing the flint to strike the steel, and the spark to ignite the tinder situated in a receptacle below the striker. The " strike a light " sometimes had a candle holder just to the fore of the tinder receptacle.

Magic Lantern

The earliest magic lantern dates from about the late 17th century. It played an important part in the home entertainment of wealthier families. In principle they have changed very little with the passage of time, but they have of course become more elegant in design. The lantern slide is often more interesting than the lantern itself. Up till the end of the 19th century, the vast majority of slides were hand painted, and by the careful use of two slides the first moving pictures were shown. Moving pictures were obtained by the use of two slides, for instance one carrying the sea, and the second one carrying a ship; these would be projected simultaneously, the slides on which the sea was painted was then agitated to give a realistic motion.

The best period for hand painted slides is undoubtedly between the 1850's and 1860's, a period roughly coinciding with the best animated slides. Animated slides were produced to give artificial fireworks, fountains with lifelike moving water, animated figures, and a host of other ingenious ideas.

Shooting Sticks

Shooting sticks are by no means a modern invention, they were certainly made during the 19th century. Some had three legs made of bent wood with a cane seat which folded for carrying, but were bulky. Another type consisted of a single stick on which the handle was unscrewed and then repositioned by another socket to form a tee shaped seat. There was also a completely wooden shooting stick that in design resembles its modern counterpart, but it was of course much heavier.

Brewing Implements

The practise of brewing one's own beer was once quite common, and implements used include hard wood shovels, and forks, mash stirrers, coopered oak sinks.

Shaving Tools

Articles connected with shaving include old razors, often encased in wooden boxes of quite elegant design, but they are also found in boxes more crudely shaped. Boxes used by barbers often contained more than one razor. Apart from the main instrument used in shaving there are many accoutrements including hones, soap boxes, wig and cravat holders, toilet cases including razor scissors, shaving brush, tooth picks, etc., and of course old shaving mugs.

There are shaving utensils in silver such as silver soap boxes, and shaving dishes, but the price of these are likely to be prohibitive.

COINS

There are more people interested in coins than in any other field of collecting. Early coins are small antiques, and their fascination stems from the fact that they have been handled by men of the past, and provide an unbroken historical record depicting past events and personages. Unlike many other antiques, they are not unique, but usually exist in sufficient quantities to provide for both large and small collector.

Collecting can be more satisfying if an attempt is made to form sets, or achieve continuity by selecting a part of a particular period, or country of origin.

It is assumed that new collectors will probably be most interested in British coins, therefore a few comments on these will be pertinent.

The subject of coin collecting has been well covered by specialist books, and a wealth of catalogues, detailing current prices, are available for the price of a stamp.

The value of coins are dependent upon their exact design, legend, mintmark, date, current demand and condition. Condition is of major importance, and for reference purposes the following grading is generally accepted in England.

FDC = Fleur-de-coin. Unused coins in a mint state, without any scratches, marks, or signs of wear.

Unc = Uncirculated. Coins as issued by the Royal Mint but due to modern methods of production, may not necessarily be perfect examples.

EF = Extremely Fine. Coins that appear to have never been in circulation, but on close examination may show very slight surface scratches or marks.

VF = Very Fine. Coins that have been little used, and only show slight traces of wear on the raised surfaces.

F   =   Fine. Weak impression due to faulty striking coins exhibiting considerable wear on their raised surfaces.

F   =   Fair. Coins on which the inscriptions and main features are still recognisable, but exhibit signs of wear.

Poor badly worn coins, not worth adding to a collection, unless, of course, they are extremely rare.

The earliest coins found in Britain were circulated some few hundred years B.C. by the migratory Belgic people from the Continent. These early coins were gold staters, designed in imitation of the stater of Philip II of Macedonia. Early in the first century A.D. some silver coins were produced in imitation of Roman examples.

First coins of the Anglo-Saxon periods (575 to 775 A.D.) were silver sceats, with designs influenced by late Roman coins, but during the 8th century, silver pennies were struck, these were made the same size and weight as the denier. A little later the weight of the silver penny was increased to 24 grains or one pennyweight. This coin was used until the 13th century, with variations in design, and the addition of a royal portrait.

From about 1279, the groat, or fourpenny piece, half-penny and farthing were included, together with coinage in gold.

During the Renaissance period, coins were made in larger denominations, in both gold and silver with designs more elegant and intricate.

Up to 1662 coins had been made by hand hammering, but this method was now abandoned and the mechanical mill and screw presses took over. Coins now became more precise and symmetrical in shape, much as they are today.

If you are contemplating the purchase of any gold coins, first acquaint yourself with the law concerned with the hoarding of gold. The Exchange Control Act of 1966, states that a collector can only hold four gold coins minted after 1837, without obtaining a licence. If you do not already have gold coins in your collection, a licence is necessary before you can buy any gold coins whatsoever.

The licence authorizes the collector to hold two gold coins of any one type minted after 1837. Coins will be considered different types if the mint marks are different, although the dates may coincide. This is not unreasonable, it does permit the collector to show both sides of any one type.

If you require a licence write to the Accounts and Dealing Dept. of the Bank of England, and they will forward an application form.

A word about cleaning coins. Providing the example is reasonable, make no attempt whatsoever to clean it, more damage is done to coins by cleaning than by any other cause. Copper coins should never be washed in water or cleaned with metal polish, any dirt in the crevices should be removed by brushing. Gold and silver coins can be carefully washed in soapy water if they are really grimy.

Do not forget that a badly cleaned coin will lose most of its value.

Would-be collectors should avail themselves of a copy of Seaby's " Standard Catalogue of British Coins ". It is a reasonably priced book which covers the period from the Belgic Migration to the present day in a very competent manner.

GLOSSARY

Aes: The term used for coins made of copper and bronze.

Blank: The blank disc of metal before it is formed between dies.

Die: Block of metal in which the design for a coin is cut, used to impress the coin blank with the actual design.

Electrum: Natural amalgam of gold and silver found in Asia Minor. The metal used for the earliest coins.

Exergue: The part of the coin below the main design, usually occupied by the date, and separated by a line.

Fabric: The metal from which a coin is manufactured, including the finish obtained by production.

Field: The flat areas on the coin surface not occupied by the design.

Flan: The complete piece of metal after striking.

Graining: The milling around the edge of a coin.

Hammered: Old method of making coins, by placing the blank between dies and hammering by hand.

Incuse: Design sunken into the surface, opposite to relief.

Inscription: Words u s u a l l y shown around the inside perimeter of a coin, but can also occupy other positions.

Legend: Another term for inscription.

Milled: Coins struck by dies operated in a coining press.

Mint-Mark: Symbol or letters on a coin indicating place where it was struck.

Mule: Non Standard coin, one that has been struck from two dies not normally used together. Sometimes a mule will have the current type on one face, and the previous type on the other face.

Obverse: The side of a coin showing the monarch's head. The principal side of a coin.

Proof: A coin specially struck from new dies, " Prooving " the dies.

Reverse: The less important side of a coin, opposite to obverse.

Stater: A piece of a given weight, usually a coin made of gold or electruse.

Struck: The term used to describe coins made from dies. The surface of such coins have a hard smooth finish.

Victorian glass.

Jug in opaque white glass.
(*Photo D. C. Gohm*)
Victorian, white strapwork, fruit basket.

FANS

Fans in one form or another, have probably been in use since the middle ages, at least in European society. In hot Eastern countries, their history will go back to Biblical times and the palm leaf.

Very few examples of European fans have been traced earlier than about 1700, and it is improbable that such examples will find their way into the hands of a new collector. Therefore, let us take a practical view of the subject and start looking at fans of the 18th and 19th century onwards.

Very early folding fans were decorated with geometric designs and simple, straight forward patterns, but the later examples became more ornamental, and depicted landscapes, scenes, and more elaboration in general design.

The functional part of a fan is called the leaf, which can be made of parchment, silk, crepe, paper, net, or gauze. The radiating arms are called " sticks " and these are usually in wood, ivory, tortoise-shell, or mother of pearl. The outer frame into which the fan was folded was called the guard, and this was usually made in the same materials as the sticks.

A variation of the conventional is known as a brise fan, the sticks have broad bladed ends, often decorated by slots and pierced designs. A coloured ribbon was threaded through a series of slots to position each blade in a slightly overlapping position with its neighbour when opened.

The most desirable fans were produced in Italy and France, in Baroque style, until about 1740.

Sticks were usually carved, or pierced, and mounted with silver piqué, this combination being a favourite method for bridle fans. During the Regency period, evening fans were small, and often decorated with spangles.

Fan leaves were often hand painted, and prior to about 1840, the painters rarely signed their work, but from 1840 onwards it became a common practice. From about

B

Fan with painted medallions on glazed paper, sticks of Mother-of-Pearl
with gold inlay. First half 19th century. Spanish?
(*Victoria and Albert Museum, Crown copyright*)

1850 to 1900, artists, both skilled and mediocre, painted
fan leaves, either professionally or just to amuse themselves. Many amateur painters turned it into a hobby.

Sticks and guards were often produced on a large scale
by cottage workers and considerable importations were
made from the Orient, which were subsequently fitted
with leaves of European design. During the early part
of the 18th century, at least in England, printed leaves
made their first appearance. These were of poor quality,
and painted cheaply, though it is not surprising since
these were considered to be expendable items, and
consequently are now relatively rare.

The collector may now have to concentrate on fans
of the Victorian era, although these cannot be compared
with 18th century examples for quality, they are never-

theless, very attractive. The fan did not play a very important part in Victorian society, they were used mainly in conjunction with evening wear.

About 1850, fans of coloured feathers became fashionable, these were known as " Cora " fans. Closely following this fashion we find fans painted in watercolours, mostly imported from France and decorated by well known artists. Lithography and hand coloured prints were used to produce fans of a cheaper quality.

Large ostrich feather fans made their appearance late in the century, and small fans of lace appliqué were still popular, but the turn of the century virtually saw the end of the fan as an item of fashion.

A rather exotic example of the 1870's was a fan made from peacock feathers. The sticks were made very delicately from ivory, and the feathers arranged so that

Fan painted on vellum, English Mid 18th century.
(*Victoria and Albert Museum, Crown copyright*)

the " eyes " of the tail feathers formed the stick terminals. The feathered leaf was finished with a hand-painted scene.

Another bewitching example is the black net fan, with sticks of blackwood painted and gilded. These were often decorated with an anecdotal scene.

Small fans, sometimes shaped like the scallop shell, had sticks of mother-of-pearl, white net leafs decorated with silver and coloured sequins.

Spanish style fans of many kinds were very popular, a typical example would have wooden sticks, painted and decorated, and a leaf of satin painted with some typical scene.

Lace was a popular leaf material, and examples using fine white Nottingham, mounted on mother-of-pearl sticks, with a painted centre panel, would now be considered a very collectable item.

It is surprising that not one British made fan was exhibited in the Great Exhibition of 1851. This must also have surprised and disappointed Queen Victoria, who in 1870 organised an Exhibition and gave a prize of £400 for the best fans. In 1878, the Worshipful Company of Fanmakers held a competition, and again 11 years later, but by now the popularity of the fan had declined beyond redemption.

FURNITURE

Just when, or how, man started to use furniture to make his existence a little more comfortable is not known, but it takes very little imagination to picture his first discovery of such chattels. A fallen tree was probably more comfortable to sit on than squatting on the ground. Sapplings laid side by side and covered with bracken must have been better to lay on than the bare earth, or the rock floor of a cave. An upturned log, or large rock would certainly provide a table, which could be used for many purposes and would be less fatiguing. This is, of course, pure conjecture, but it is a fact that man did know and understood how to use timber well before historic records were produced.

Furniture of a high standard has been found in the tombs of Ancient Egypt, dating back to about 2600 B.C. These excellent examples produced with the relatively crude tools of adze, axe, saw, chisel, mallet and hammer, show the high degree of skill of the craftsman, and the advanced stage in the evolution of furniture.

The evolution of furniture provides an interesting historical study.

The collector can pursue this study at his leisure if he so desires, but it is unlikely to be rewarding in terms of actual collecting, therefore we will concentrate our attention to more recent periods.

The predominant timber during Tudor times was oak, and the furniture generally heavy in construction. Early Tudor examples are austere in design, as it was not a period when furniture was considered very important. Owners of large houses only boasted the bare essentials of bed, table, stool, bench, and chests for general storage purposes. Chairs were limited to the master and mistress of the household. Such was the poverty of furniture, that chests generally used for storage were often pressed into use for seats, tables, and beds. Chests, coffers and chairs with high backs were often carved.

Early Tudor furniture is not for the collector, but it

Two Tea Caddies, mahogany and rosewood, brass inlay and mounts.
C. 1750.
(*Victoria and Albert Museum, Crown copyright*)

can be seen in museums, and perhaps some old country houses.

Up to the 15th century, furniture was constructed rather crudely with planks and pegs, the planks slotted into end frames and then pegged, but this method was superseded early in this period by the innovation of joinery techniques involving the mortise and tenon. These techniques were not the perfect examples later produced by the cabinet-maker, but neverthless a real step forward.

During the reign of Henry VIII the middle classes found themselves with money to spend. This resulted in an increase in the building of private houses with a corresponding increased demand for and supply of furniture. Henry encouraged immigrant foreign crafts-men to England, who brought with them the styles of the classical Renaissance, which slowly replaced the Gothic designs and motifs.

The Elizabethan period increased the sophistication with French and Italian influences, carvings of swages of

Armchair. Satinwood with painted decoration. English, second half 19th century.
(*Victoria and Albert Museum, Crown copyright*)

fruit, eagles, medallions, and strap-work were used in rich ornamentation.

Oak was still the predominant timber.

The gate-leg table was a Jacobean innovation, and table tops which until this time had been mostly rectangular became oval or round. It was a period that moved away from the heavy styles of the Tudor and Elizabethan periods into lighter and more elegant designs, and Oriental lacquer work made its appearance,

Armchair, Beech carved in relief and painted black with gilt details.
Lion design in Regency style. C. 1810.
(*Victoria and Albert Museum, Crown copyright*)

but mainly by importations. Metal workers joined forces with the furniture makers, and handles of simple design in both brass and wrought iron were added.

Late Stuart furniture was greatly influenced by the immigrant foreign craftsmen who returned with Charles II and his Court from exile.

Much of the best London examples were made by these craftsmen, who introduced techniques that were in use on the Continent, such as gilding, lacquering, marquetry and veneering.

Walnut superseded oak as the most desirable material, and continued to be favoured for about seventy years until mahogany took its place.

Joinery had ceased to be an undeveloped method, it blossomed into a true craft that was practised by joiner and cabinet maker alike. English workers also had the opportunity of furthering their skills by studying Oriental workmanship. Inlay work was executed on many articles of furniture with a precision and delicacy that had not been possible previously. Inlaid materials included ivory, bone, ebony and hollywood.

Cabinets which were a development of early chests, became very sophisticated and artistic, with secret compartments and drawers, which are the delight of modern collectors.

The well established cabriole leg was a feature of the William and Mary period, the general shape was a flattened ' S ' with a section that tapered from thick top to a thin foot. It was not an English design but came to us from Holland. In fact much of the furniture of this period was strongly influenced by the Dutch cabinet-makers, who gave us curved tied stretchers for chairs, and dome-topped cabinets. The timber in current use was still walnut, which was now increasingly enriched by designers, in marquetry, again the result of Dutch craftsmen.

During the next period, Queen Anne, the English craftsmen made full use of the skills and ingeniousness that they had learned from their foreign counterparts, and proceeded to use these skills to produce excellent quality furniture, but with English styles. The cabriole leg, still very much in vogue, was ornamented at the outward curve, or knee, by shell carvings or carved heads. Chair legs which until now had been strengthened by stretchers, became unsupported, and the splat, that is the panel situated in the centre of the back, became highly decorated with carvings. This period also saw the introduction of the Windsor chair, with plain wooden seat and the lath back.

Mahogany, imported from Cuba and Honduras, was introduced during the reign of George I. It was not until somewhat later during the early Georgian period that the timber was established as a successor to the then prevailing walnut. Oak, beech and chestnut were still in use, but to a lesser extent.

The Georgian period, which covers the majority of the 18th century, was a period when form became more important than ornamentation. The cabriole leg was developed to perfection by such masters as Chippendale. The term " Chippendale " has become synonymous with the style of furniture from this period, but it does not necessarily mean that the examples were actually produced in his workshops. Original Chippendale carvings are clean, deep, and crisp, and it is well worth visiting a museum or country house to see some of his work so that you *know* the real thing. Chippendale was not the only designer to gain a reputation—Ince and Mayhew, Edwards and Darley, William Vile, William Hamelt, and Mannaring and Johnson, were just a few of his rivals.

The Regency period is probably best noted for its " Neo-Classic Style " of furniture, which in fact copied the furniture of classical times. The inspiration came from Pompeii, in Italy, where archaeologists were excavating examples of historic interest, and from Greco-Roman designs. The Regency period was an unsettled artistic period, with new forms of expression being continually sought. Designers used Egyptian, Chinese, and Gothic styles in addition to the Greco-Roman. Egyptian

Sofa-table, Mahogany with ebony enrichments. C. 1820.
(*Victoria and Albert Museum, Crown copyright*)

motifs found on furniture are serpents, lion supports, lotus leaves and sphinx heads.

Chinese furniture was largely japanned and decorated with mandarins and other Oriental motifs.

Inlaying with brass was a feature of the period, it had the decorativeness of marquetry, the advantages of lasting longer, and gave a quality finish.

Victorian furniture is noted for its flamboyant ornamentation, abundance of curves, and rounded corners. Favourite woods were rosewood and mahogany, and to some extent oak. It was a period of expansion, both in population, and products to satisfy their needs. Mass production in a modern sense, did not really get under way until later in the 19th century, although some machines were employed to produce carving, and for

Pole-screen, carved mahogany, with a panel of embroidery in silks, wool and silver gilt thread. Style of Chippendale. First half of 18th century. (*Victoria and Albert Museum, Crown copyright*)

limited other jobs. The extra demands on the furniture industry were met by the simple expedient of employing more workers.

The history of furniture is, of course, a long and complicated subject, and from a collector's viewpoint, best studied either in periods, or by tracing the history of a particular interest, such as chairs or similar small pieces. A general, but by no means precise guide to the three divisions into which furniture can be classified is as follows:—

Up to about 1650 — " Age of Oak "
From about 1650 to 1750 " Age of Walnut "
From about 1750 — " Age of Mahogany ".

Large furniture is not a very convenient subject for the small collector of antiques, it is far better suited to museums who have the space to display the articles to advantage, and also the means to purchase them. If, however, one is so inclined it is possible to use antique furniture for one's home, and at the same time to consider the pieces as part of a collection. This gives the best of two worlds. An obvious advantage of such an arrangement is the fact that, unlike modern furniture, its re-sale value will almost certainly be in excess of the original purchase price, should you wish to dispose of it in the future.

VICTORIAN CHAIRS

Smokers Bow

So named because it was a favourite of the smoking room, and had a bow back. This was formed by a thick semi-circular piece of wood supported from the solid wooden seat by either seven or eight turned spindles. The legs were beautifully turned and strengthened by turned double stretchers. As the period developed, the legs and spindles became less ornamental.

The shape of this chair also made it suitable for barbers shops and public houses.

Fan-back Windsor

The back of this chair was designed with two turned supports on the outside, and rails in between, which were set into a circular seat, and tapered outwards until they met the straight top rail. This gave the fan shape.

Legs were turned and supported by turned stretchers.

The Fan-back Windsor chair was in use during the late 18th century, and was made throughout the Victorian period, with minor modifications in turning and top rail.

Lath and Baluster Windsor

This was a heavy solid wooden armchair with turned baluster legs, and double cross-stretchers. The seat was solid wood, with a back made from curved laths, and decorative splat. Splat decorated usually by cutting the wide piece of wood into an attractive shape, i.e. not carved. Arms supported on turned baluster pillars. Woods used were beech, and often stained to imitate rosewood, or painted.

Lady's Easy Chair

The back and seat of this chair was virtually made in one piece, supported by a curved continuous frame not unlike a modern slatted garden chair.

Legs were curved, and each pair connected with a single turned stretcher. The chair, which was without any arm rests, was low and comfortable, and it had the advantage of permitting the voluminous skirts worn by women to drape naturally, unrestricted by arm rest supports.

This chair was made during the first half of the Victorian period, but the shape originated in Regency times.

Papier Mâché Chair

Papier mâché was not quite so successful structurally for furniture as the furniture makers had hoped. Victorian papier mâché chairs are invariably made with wooden legs and frame to overcome this deficiency.

These chairs were beautifully japanned and decorated with gilding, mother-of-pearl inlay, and the backs were sometimes painted with beautiful views. (For description of techniques employed in producing papier mâché see appropriate heading.)

Balloon-back Chairs

Balloon-back chairs were used for the drawing room, bedroom, and dining room. They were a very popular shape until about the middle of the period, and they were still being made up to about 1890, although not in such large quantities.

The back of the chair had a curved top that " waisted in " as it approached the seat, the outline somewhat resembling the shape of a balloon in flight. Seats were usually upholstered, the legs were the usual cabriole style, but after about 1850 drawing room chairs had French style cabriole legs. Early balloon-backs did not have such pronounced waisting, or cabriole legs. The rear legs were often part of the back, and front legs were turned balusters.

Spoon-back Chair

Spoon backs were invariably small upholstered chairs without arm rests. The name spoon back refers to the spoon like shape of the back, which to some extent follows the shape of the human back. It was usual to upholster these chairs with Berlin woolwork.

Morris Adjustable-back Chair

Designed as an easy chair for the drawing room, it

had an adjustable bar at the back to alter the angle of recline. The back consisted of a wooden frame, supporting a separate squab, the seat had its own separate cushion and the arms were upholstered. Castors were often fitted to all legs. This design became so popular in America, that chairs of similar design are still known as " Morris chairs ".

Easy Chair

The early easy chair was made with a mahogany frame. Seat, back and filled in padded arm rests were upholstered. Back and arm rest sides were deeply buttoned. Original upholstery material was usually leather, but other materials were used.

Later in the period, easy chairs were made to appear lighter by removing the upholstery from between the arm rest and seat, and replacing it with turned wooden spindles. Leather was still the popular covering, and horse-hair the common padding material.

Bentwood Rocker

Bentwood furniture was produced by bending strips of beech, made pliable under steam, to form the frame. The particular rocking chair, made by Thonet, of Vienna. had a light bentwood framework, to support the back and seat. Strips of wood were carried down and under to form the curved rocking members. The bentwood rocker was the product of mass production techniques.

Children's Chairs

Many chairs were designed specifically for small children. Solid little rocking chairs with turned rocker supports and arm rests. Sturdy little balloon-backs with curved arms and upholstered seats, and tall, slim chairs in bamboo, and many other attractive miniature examples of adult furniture.

REGENCY CHAIRS
Rope Back, or Trafalgar Chair

The Rope Back was a Grecian style dining chair, so named because the back centre bar was often made to

Armchair, Beechwood, carved, japanned and partly gilded, upholstered
in modern silk. C. 1810.
(*Victoria and Albert Museum, Crown copyright*)

represent a twisted rope. The rope, having marine
connections, is obviously responsible for its other name,
Trafalgar. The general design was clean with plain
curved legs, and back stiles very slightly curved
terminating in a scroll.

The slat forming the top rail was often embellished
with brass inlay.

Hope's X back Chair

This is another chair that was based on ancient Grecian designs. Both front and rear legs were curved strikingly outwards, forming a shape known as " sabre leg ". The back stiles were ornamented with a concave top rail that extended beyond the stiles, and a further support joined the two stiles just above the upholstered seat, forming a rectangular space. Into this space, two curved pieces of wood were mounted, back to back, to create the " X " shape. Thomas Hope, who was responsible for the design of this chair, was a wealthy banker and antiquary. His work " Household Furniture and Interior Decoration " was published in 1807, and undoubtedly his designs greatly influenced the taste of the period.

Hope's Chairs

Early period pieces illustrated in his " Household Furniture " were strongly classical, usually with boldly curved sabre legs. One of his styles shows a carved sphinx supporting one end of a straight arm rest, the other end joining the curved back stiles about half way up. Top rail, wide, but of a simple design, is extended beyond the stiles. Another typical design, again sabre legged, has a slightly curved back, radiusing at the bottom and curving into the seat, making the back and seat a one piece construction. Front side, and back top of the frame terminates in scroll-work.

Carver's Chair

The " carver " is an armchair and, as its name suggests, it was used at table by the person carving the meat.

Early period carvers had sabre legs but not so bold as Hope's. The arm rests swept down from the back stiles to end in a semi-circle, similar to the end of a scroll. The lower part of the scroll was fixed directly to the seat frame.

Top rail was often fitted with a brass handle to facilitate the handling of the chair, and it was often decorated, most attractively, with brass inlay.

A weakness in the design was caused by the cross grain of the wood used in making the curved arms, due to cutting these from a single plank.

Library Chair

The Library Chair was an interesting example with a dual purpose. It could be sat on or quickly converted into steps for reaching the higher shelves in the library.

This chair had one end of the curved arm rests fixed directly to the seat frame, the other joining the back supports about half way up. The top rail was slightly curved, otherwise quite plain. The squab-type seat, arms and back were made in one piece and hinged along the front edge, so that by standing in front of the chair and pulling the back towards you, the seat and back described an arc until the top rail rested on the floor, to expose four steps.

George Smith Armchair

This style of armchair was fashionable for a few years early in the 19th century when anything Egyptian was in vogue. The most distinctive feature of this style was the front legs which were designed and carved to resemble the legs of animals, including terminations with a complete hoof. The front legs were extended and carried up to form the front supports to the padded arm rests, which were most ebaborately carved. Other decorations often incorporated were griffins and sphinxes in brass.

George Smith was a cabinet maker, who published a design book in 1808 entitled " A Collection of Designs for Household Furniture and Interior Decorating ". In this book he showed examples based on studies of ancient Egyptian, Greek and Roman styles.

GEORGIAN CHAIRS

Comb-back Windsor

The Comb-back Windsor is an attractive country armchair. Like most Windsors the seat was solid and slightly hollowed to fit the buttocks. The simple tapering legs were inserted into holes under the seat and stretcher-less.

The tall back was made with thin rods, topped by a simple rail. Both arm rests were formed from a single, curved, wooden member, supported by short double tapered rods on the sides. The back rods passed through holes in the rear of the arm-rest and terminated in sockets in the seat.

A later version of the comb-back had turned legs, strengthened by stretchers, the back rods tapered from a shaped top rail into the seat giving a fan shape, and the arm rests, although still made from a single curved member, were not filled in with rods. They were supported by two simple lath-like struts.

Hoop-back Windsor

The hoop-back of this chair was made from a single piece of wood, bent to form a rough inverted horse-shoe. The two ends of the " horse shoe " fitted into two holes in the seat, forming a framework that was later filled with wooden rods. Arm rests were made from separate pieces of wood, fixed to the back frame, and supported at the tips by curved members connected to the seat.

The seat of solid wood had a rectangular projection at the rear from which two diagonally positioned struts supported the back near the top.

Wheel-back Windsor

Generally followed the design of Windsor Comb-back chairs except that the legs were turned and supported by stretchers, and it had a back formed from a bentwood frame, instead of a top rail and stiles. The most distinctive feature of this chair was the removal of the central rods from the back, and the introduction of a shaped and fretted splat, the motif of which was a spoked wheel, hence the name, " Wheel-back ".

Ladder-back

The ladder-back comes mainly from the northern part of England. The back framework was made by an extension of the rear legs, forming stiles that were con-

Armchair, Ash Ladder back with rush seat, designed and made by Ernest Simpson. C. 1888.
(*Victoria and Albert Museum, Crown copyright.*)

nected by horizontal slats, either plain or shaped. Front legs also were extended above the seat to support one end of the arm rest. The seat proper consisted of a frame, more often than not rush filled.

Adam Shield-back

As the name suggests, the back of this very elegant chair was shield-shape. The seat was upholstered, and the back padded to leave an outer frame of wood, which emphasised the outline. Rear legs were relatively plain, but the front legs were fluted and carved in a distinctly French classical style. Robert Adam (1728–92), the designer, was trained originally as an architect by his father, he spent some years travelling and studying on the continent, and although, no doubt, an excellent architect, it is his work in connection with classical style interior decoration, that his name will be generally associated.

Spindle-back

The Spindle-back has much in common with the ladder-back. The extensions of the front legs forming the arm rest supports were turned baluster shape. The back main frame was made from extensions of the rear legs supported by members or rails. In between these cross members, rows of turned spindles were inserted. The spindles were either equally spaced in rows, or bunched towards the centre, and sometimes a combination of both methods were used.

VICTORIAN SMALL TABLES

Work Tables

There were, of course, many styles and types of work table. One particular style in vogue about 1840 had an inlaid chequered board on the top obviously for chess and draughts. The octagonal table top was hinged to permit access to the interior compartments which held sewing materials. The compartment in the middle had no bottom, but it had suspended below it a bag made of Berlin woolcloth.

The top was supported by four curved pieces of wood which met under the table and joined a central ornate pillar, this pillar was mounted on a cross-shaped piece of wood, the four points of which carried castors and was heavily ornamented with scroll carvings.

Wood used for this very elegant table was invariably walnut.

Later Victorian work tables were of a similar basic design, but were often simpler, with a tripod base, and an inverted tripod supporting the top. The woolwork bag was replaced by a pierced work " basket " but bags were still used made in pleated silk and soft leather.

Pembroke Table

These tables were supposedly named after the lady who first ordered one. They were first used about 1760, and they were known also as breakfast tables.

The table was either rectangular or rounded and had two small hinged flaps which were held in position by two swinging wooden brackets. Often had drawers fitted, and legs without stretchers.

Sutherland Table

The Sutherland table was virtually a small gate-leg table. Any advantage this design may have had over the Pembroke is the fact that it folded quite small, but when folded, it tended to be unstable. It had four turned main legs terminating in two blocked shaped feet. Hinged flaps were held in position by two legs which swung out from the main frieze, or apron.

Sofa Table

This was a small, invariably narrow, table, with two drawers in the apron. Each end of the table had a small flap. The legs were either fitted one at each corner, or the table was supported on trestle-like brackets, connected by stretchers half way up, or low down near the floor.

Occasional Tables

An occasional table is a light, easily portable, small table that can be moved to suit any occasion. There were a great number and variety of such tables produced during the Victorian period.

REGENCY SMALL TABLES

Sofa Tables

Sofa Tables of the Regency period were very elegant. The Pedestal Sofa Table had four legs meeting at a pedestal support, with feet of brass claws and castors. The single pedestal sat on the pedestal support and the table on the pedestal. The overall design was classical, and decorated with brass.

The Sheraton Sofa Table, somewhat simpler in design, had the usual two flaps, and two shallow drawers. Legs were formed by two inverted " Y " shaped trestles, strengthened by an ornately turned stretcher.

Average size of sofa tables were approximately five to six feet long, and two feet wide. These tables were generally used in the library, drawing room, and any ladies' apartment.

Side Tables

Side or pier tables were generally used in the dining room. There were many designs, and it was common to support the table by lion monopodia or by Egyptian figures and mythical creatures. Some styles had a platform near the base fitted with silvered glass to reflect objects placed on it.

The tops of some side tables were made from solid marble, and elegantly ornamented with brass inlay and applied brass motifs.

Dumbwaiters

Dumbwaiters were a firm favourite of the Regency house who used them mainly for dessert. There were many designs, but the majority were two or three tiered structures, mounted on a centred column terminating in a base from which three or four legs curved downwards to brass lion foot castors. The circular tiers rotated to simplify selection of the various sweetmeats placed on them.

Loo Tables

Loo tables were used in the drawing room as games tables, in fact their name was derived from a card game popular during the period.

It was a circular table supported on a single ornate pedestal from which three or four curved ornate legs were mounted.

GEORGIAN SMALL TABLES

Neo-Classic Tripod

These were useful little tables especially those that made provision for hinging the top into a vertical position. This feature made it easy to store, and displayed the inlaid or painted top to advantage.

The tripod legs were surmounted with a single pedestal which supported the top.

Tea Table

It was customary, about the middle of the 18th century, to provide a table for each person taking tea. These tables were generally little tripod affairs with a circular top that tilted for storage. Around the edge of the top was either a pie crust moulding or a delicate little brass rail, known as a gallery, to prevent the china from slipping off.

Concertina Card Table

This table was a most interesting development about the middle of the period. It could be used as a side table, or opened out for card playing.

A typical example of this table would have a hinged flap top that folded back on itself when used as a side table. The cabriole legs were beautifully carved, and terminated with a ball and claw foot. The frieze supporting the top had two hinged sections either side that folded like a section of a concertina bellows. To increase the table size it was only necessary to pull the two front legs forward, and fold over the hinged top, like opening a book.

Eagle Tables

Eagle tables will not be found easily, and even if one should turn up it will be much too expensive for the average collector. However, these tables are much too interesting to be omitted on that account.

Basically, the table consists of a large carved eagle with outstretched wings, its clawed feet gripping a rectangular plinth. The top, often made of marble, was supported on the eagle's head and wings . The eagle was invariably gilded, and when set off with a black marble top, and imitation black marble plinth, the overall effect was most extravagant and lavish.

Georgian houses would often use this type of table in conjunction with a mirror, but it is almost certain that you will have to visit a stately home to see one today.

MISCELLANEOUS ITEMS

VICTORIAN

Fire Screens

Fire Screens were first known in England during the 18th century, but it was the Victorians who popularised this decorative piece of furniture by featuring it in almost every room containing a fire place.

One type, popular early in the period consisted of a single pole supported either by tripod legs or a round base. The actual screen was usually made of a needlework panel or a decorated wooden panel, which could be adjusted up and down to protect the face from the heat of the fire. The tripod legs, and base of the upright pole were often decorated with carvings. The most commonly used embroidery was Berlin wool work, those with Soho tapestry are rare, and practically unobtainable. Papier mâché pole screens were a great favourite. These were most artistically made, and decorated with landscapes and figures, or with Chinoiserie designs and gilding.

Tea Containers

Tea, the British national drink, was an expensive luxury when it was first introduced over 300 years ago, so it is not surprising that it was treated with some reverence, and stored in silver canisters which were kept in a box, later known as tea chests.

A typical Victorian teapoy is virtually a tea caddy on legs. Generally made in mahogany, with an ornate pedestal legged base. The top consisted of a thick circular box with a lid, which, when opened, exposed one or two fitted tea canisters.

Early Victorian teapoys were usually rectangular, and often inlaid with mother-of-pearl. Later examples were made in a variety of shapes.

Teapoys made in papier mâché were made throughout most of the Victorian period, usually beautifully japanned and decorated. Collectors usually seek examples with finely painted landscapes on the inside of the lid, but these are now quite rare.

Tea Caddies of various shapes, and tea-chests of various woods decorated with marquetry, make useful, collectable items.

Other items

Victorian trays were made in a tremendous variety. Small circular " waiters " for presenting a glass of wine, rectangular, oval and curved fronted, examples were made in wood and papier mâché and used for a number of special purposes.

Other collectable items include music stools, knife boxes, wine cisterns, stands for vases, basins, kettles, and small display cabinets.

REGENCY

Tea Containers

The teapoy was a Regency invention developed originally from a simple three legged table used about 1750 as an individual table for persons taking tea. Later in the century this custom slowly disappeared, and the tables were then used to stand the tea caddies on. The final stage of development was the incorporation of both caddies and table to make the teapoy.

A typical late Regency teapoy would be made in rosewood, perhaps with four strongly curved legs, terminated with brass lions claws and castors. The pedestal, often rectangular in section, would have an ornamented profile and would support a rectangular chest. Brass inlay was often used as a decorative design feature, but mother-of-pearl was also used.

A late Regency teapoy to be seen in the Victoria and Albert Museum is made in rosewood, it has four relatively plain legs, supporting a plain pedestal base. The turned pedestal supports a chest, under which is hung a tasselled semi-circular half barrel.

Dwarf Bookcase

This small type of portable bookcase was a new fashion that first appeared in Regency times. It consisted of a case, usually in rosewood, supported by a beautifully turned pedestal at each end. The pedestals sat on a pair of " Y " feet, strengthened with a single turned stretcher. The front doors were either glazed or fitted with a brass wire trellis, and a shelf provided for two rows of books.

Dwarf bookcases were low pieces of furniture designed to leave ample wall space above them for hanging pictures.

Another innovation of the period was the revolving bookcase—legs supported a central shaft on which the bookcases were fixed in such a way that they could be rotated at will. Shapes were either round, rectangular or any other compatible shape.

An interesting development of the " bookcase " evolved a most attractive little Regency piece—the set of portable open shelves, the sides of which were often made of brass wire. These shelves were designed so that " my lady " could carry it easily about the house, when moving from one room to another.

Canterbury

The Canterbury is a rack for holding sheet music. It is suggested that the name originated as a result of an Archbishop of Canterbury ordering the first one.

It consisted of an openwork, rectangular box structure with divisions for music books, and usually had a drawer underneath for sheet music. It was supported on each corner by a turned and castored leg, which made it an easy matter to push it under the piano keyboard when not in use.

GLOSSARY

Acanthus: A foliage or leaf design originally adorning Corinthian capitals, but later adapted as a design motif in furniture. The design was used by Chippendale on the knees of cabriole legs.

Art Nouveau: This was a style of furniture used at the turn of the 19th century, it was stiff with a tendency towards vertical lines.

Baluster: A pillar usually turned, to support a rail.

Baroque: Refers to the late Renaissance period, when decoration became flamboyant with scrolls and natural motifs.

Beading: A small usually semi-circular moulding, used to form a ridge or decoration on furniture.

Bail: A drawer fitting comprising a half loop of metal, usually brass, fitted to drawers by metal bolts.

Barley Sugar or Twist Turning: A form of turning resembling the twist in barley sugar or the effect of twisting two ropes together.

Bell Flower: A decorative motif consisting of a stylised flower with three or five petals hanging downwards. It was often used as a carving or inlaid in a series, one below the other, also known as Husk motif.

Bracket: A bracket fixed to the wall usually for displaying ornaments or busts.

Cabinet: A piece of furniture, glass fronted, intended for displaying porcelain or other artistic pieces.

Cabinet Making: Craft of furniture making requiring skill of a high order employing joinery and engineering techniques.

Cabriole Leg: The shape of a leg used almost universally in the 18th century. It has a slow curve like a flattened ' S ', representational of the animal form. The foot of the leg terminated in various designs including the claw and ball foot, slipper foot, the pad, and the scroll in the Chippendale style.

Canted: Tipped at an angle.

Carpentry: The m a k i n g of wooden structures not requiring the skill of the cabinet maker, and uniting timbers with the use of nails.

Caryatid: An upright carved in the human form.

Cheval-Glass: A large rectangular mirror which pivoted in a frame work, or moved up and down within the frame. Usually supported on four legs.

Chiffonier: Originally t h i s meant a tall chest of drawers, but used to describe a low cupboard during the Regency period.

Chip-Carving: A method of carving used for surface ornamentation, motifs developed by lightly chipping away the wood.

Claw-and-Ball foot: Used on terminations of legs, for chairs and other pieces of furniture. Originally believed to have been adapted from the Chinese dragons claw holding a pearl.

Coffer: Coffers are often confused with chests, in fact, they are a chest but the definition demands that they should be covered with some material such as leather, and banded with metalwork.

Cresting: Ornament on the top or crest of a structure sometimes shaped, carved or perforated, as seen in the cresting of a chair.

Daventry: A small chest of drawers with an angled top used for writing.

Dentils: A decoration used beneath the moulding of a cornice representing a series of small rectangles.

Dowel: A wooden peg used for joining two pieces of wood together or for positioning same.

Ebonise: To imitate ebony. This was accomplished by staining the wood.

Fillet: A small narrow strip of wood, usually flat.

Finial: The top decoration, usually a knob situated on the top of posts. Often seen on chair uprights.

Fluting: A classical style decoration involving narrow vertical grooves reminiscent of classical architecture. Often used on straight legs.

Gadrooning: A style of decoration used for edgings in carving. The pattern is formed of straight or radiating lines with raised lobes between the lines.

Inlay: Decoration formed by letting in separate pieces of different coloured materials, such as woods, ivories, tortoise shell, bone, etc., into a recessed base.

Japanning: A technique which became popular in England during the late 17th century, it is a lacquered finish obtained by the use of gums and spirits.

Joinery: Woodwork that has been made using specialist joints such as the mortise and tenon and dovetail.

Linenfold: A carved ornamentation suggestive of folded linen.

Marquetry: A method of decoration involving the process of inlaying woods and other materials into a veneer.

Melon-bulb: The large, melon like swelling on legs or posts of furniture. Usually elaborately carved.

Moulding: Ornamental strip of wood used to enclose panels, or to finish the edge of a lid and for many other purposes.

Ogee: A double curved moulding or support. The top is convex in shape and changes to concave below.

Ormolu: An alloy of copper, zinc and tin resembling gold, gilt bronze. A preparation of gold leaf used for gilding furniture.

Patina: In furniture, this refers to the finish of the woodwork, the beautiful soft gloss on antique, well cared for furniture.

Pier Table: A table designed to stand between two windows, i.e. the pier. Loosely used to describe any table that has been designed to stand against a wall.

Rail: This is the top member of a chair, supported by the styles. It is also any horizontal piece of framing or panelling.

Reeding: This is a very similar decoration to fluting but in this instance the ornamentation is in relief representing a series of slim reeds.

Rococo: A florid and asymmetrical style of decoration using rocks and shells as the motif. It was developed in France from Chinese forms and came to England between 1730 and 1780.

Rush Seat: A seat made of woven rushes, mostly used on country furniture.

Sabre Leg: Sabre shaped, describes the sharply curving leg of the classical style.

Saddle Seat: Resembling a saddle. Solid wooden seats as used in Windsor chairs, which have been shaped somewhat to suit the buttocks and in doing so roughly resemble the seat of a saddle.

Settle: Usually refers to seats with a boxed base, an earlier stage of the settee.

Splat: The upright member in the middle of the back of a chair, often decorated by carving and fretting.

Stile: The upright side pieces of a piece of furniture, usually the outermost.

Strapwork: A band or ornamentation representative of plated straps. Strapwork is usually stylised.

Straw-work: The forming of landscapes and geometrical patterns by the use of tiny strips of bleached pink coloured straws. This method of decoration came to England towards the end of the 17th century from the Continent and was used mainly for small pieces of furniture.

Stretcher: The horizontal members connecting legs of chairs and other vertical members of furniture.

Stump Leg: A short thick rear leg slightly curved.

Tunbridge Ware: A form of inlay developed in Tunbridge Wells about 1650. The process used minute strips of wood of many natural colours to build up patterns. Early examples were mainly of geometrical designs but later landscapes and floral decorations were used to decorate boxes, tea-caddies, trays, etc.

Turning: This is a method of shaping wood with cutting tools whilst the wood is rotating in a lathe.

What-not: A type of rack used from about 1800 onwards for books and ornaments. It is a series of shelves supported by four uprights.

GLASS

The history of early glass making is obscure. There is no evidence to show when it was discovered, or how it was discovered. The Egyptians had mastered the methods of making glass more than 3500 years ago, and from fragments found it is not unreasonable to suppose that this was the first ever made. It is known that the Egyptians made beads and small amulets some 2000 years B.C.

The Egyptians produced hollow vessels by shaping molten glass either around cores of sand, or by dipping the cores repeatedly into the molten glass; they also pressed molten glass into open moulds. Glass blowing, the method of shaping hot glass by blowing down a hollow rod, was discovered some 2000 years ago and opened the way for producing glass in more elegant forms.

From these early beginnings glass has gone through the usual process of refinement in both design and methods used to attain better results.

Hollow vessels, such as wine glasses, relied very much on the skill of the glass blower up to the late 17th century, and a brief description of the methods employed may be of interest.

Molten glass is a hot, sticky mass, that readily adheres to the hollow iron blow rod or to itself. The blow rod was dipped into the molten mass until sufficient glass adhered to the tip, then it was withdrawn and rolled to and fro on a flat surface to remove any lumps. The next stage was to blow down the rod to expand the molten glass into a bubble of the desired size; this was ascertained by checking with calipers, or with some other suitable gauge. A blob of glass was then added to the end of the bowl and the stem forged. The foot was then added in the same way and shaped, whilst being rotated, with a pair of wooden boards.

A second rod was then temporarily attached to the foot with a dab of molten glass, to hold the glass whilst the mouth was cut from the blow pipe with a wetted metal tool at a position where the rim was required. Any rough edge on the bowl was trimmed with shears and smoothed by fire polishing, which was achieved by reheating in a furnace. The final operation was to break off the second rod which had only been necessary as a means of holding the wine glass during the latter operation. The rough marks produced by the break is known as the pontil mark.

During the majority of the foregoing operations it was necessary to continually rotate the wine glass on the end of the blow pipe, during its manufacture. This was executed by the " gaffer " who sat in a chair with extended arm rests. The rod was rolled to and fro along the arm rests to keep the glass in constant rotation and to prevent it from sagging under its own weight. It must also be remembered that thin sections of glass cool rapidly, with consequent loss of plasticity, therefore, if the operation was a lengthy one, the glass had to be continually reheated in between operations, to retain its workability.

Glass moulding is a very old process. Early glass articles were formed by pressing the molten glass into moulds made from stone or clay, and any patterning required was obtained by cutting the pattern into the mould so that when the glass was pressed into the grooves, the pattern appeared on the finished product in cameo, i.e. raised glass.

So that the moulds could be used more than once, the articles had to be designed so that they were easily withdrawn, no undercutting was permitted that prevented their easy removal. Roman glass workers added a decoration called Pillar moulding, this was a raised ribbing, executed by means of lifting the still plastic glass by means of pincers.

With the advent of glass blowing, moulded glass could take another step forward. The moulds were now made in two or three pieces in such a way that they could be broken apart for the removal of the specimen.

Print "The Great Atlantic Race", lithographed and painted by T. G. Dutton. Published 1967.

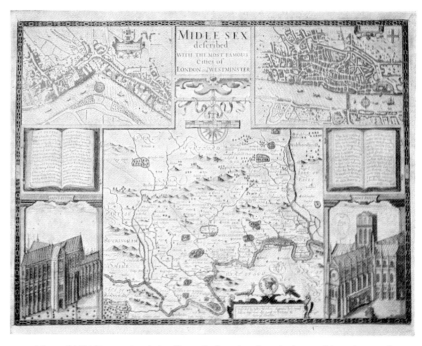

Map of Middlesex by John Speed showing inset plans of London and Westminster, and views of St. Peters and St. Pauls. Published C. 1616.

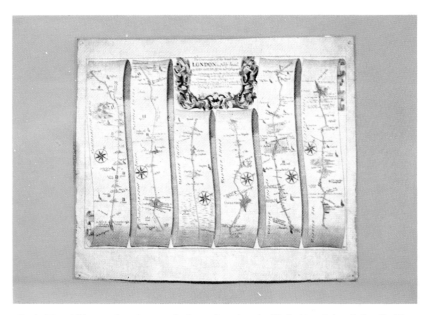

Early Road Maps showing route from London to Holy Head, by John Ogilby. Published 1670.
(Parker Gallery)

The glass blower proceeded much in the same way as if he was making our wine glass, that is, he inserted his hollow iron blowing rod into the molten mass of glass so that a gob formed on the end, then with successive emersions into the molten glass, he would increase the gob in size until there was sufficient to make the required article. The plastic lump of glass was then rolled onto a cast iron plate or a smooth stone until the mass was worked to the end of the tube, the pear shape gob of glass was then inserted into the mould and blown. The gob expanded like a balloon inside the mould and took up the form of the mould. If the article being manufactured was a bulbous item like a bottle, the two or three parts of the mould could be opened and the bottle withdrawn. Should further work be necessary, the pontil rod would have been added to the bottom of the article with a dab of molten glass for finishing.

As the thickness of the bubble of glass is more or less consistent the finished article would therefore have the same shape both externally and internally, except that bumps on the outside will be depressions on the inside.

Pressed glass should not be confused with moulded glass. A large proportion of Victorian glass was produced by pressing, a process thought to have originated in the United States of America during the late 1820's.

The principles of pressing glass involved the use of a mould, which consisted of a block of metal that had been hollowed out to comply with the exterior shape of the article to be produced. If the article was larger in girth than at its apex, the mould would be split into two or four parts so that the finished article could be removed.

Molten glass was dropped into the mould cavity and a top tool; or follower, was pressed into the glass; this forced the glass to take up the shape of the mould interior, thus forming the outside shape. The top tool or follower provided the inside shape. Therefore it will be seen that with pressed glass the interior shape and exterior shape can be quite different. Facetted on the outside, smooth on the interior.

C

Pressed glass gives a much sharper definition than blown moulded specimens due to the higher pressure used, and they can be produced at a much faster rate.

The introduction of pressed glass during Victorian times heralded the first stages of mechanization in the glass industry.

The machines required for bringing the two halves of the mould together were relatively cheap, and because of their relatively high output, articles made of glass were produced much cheaper than hitherto.

During the process of manufacture, both pressed and moulded glass required finishing and annealing, which was executed by fire polishing at the furnace mouth, simultaneously with the annealing process. Pressed glass made after 1850 rarely shows any trace of a pontil mark as from that date onwards a spring clip was used to remove the articles from the mould.

Although both pressed and blown moulded glass are formed and patterned by the use of moulds, there is a difference that can be detected by the collector. It has already been said that pressed glass has a stronger and better defined pattern. If we now look at the mould marks, that is the thin lines reproduced on the articles from the segments of the mould, we will find that those from blown moulding are very faint, due to the relatively small pressures that have been used in blowing. Because of the forces exerted in the press were very great by comparison these mould marks tend to be better defined. As the pressure built up in the mould, there was a tendency to force the sections apart, which tended to increase the size of the mould mark.

Pressed glass was used extensively from about 1840 to 1860 for the production of general goods, such as dishes, drinking glass and the usual household paraphernalia, and these can be bought quite reasonably.

Glass cutting is a familiar method of decoration, the angled patterns and facets produced give a prismatic effect when light is reflected on their many surfaces, causing the glass to glow and sparkle with colours of the

Nailsea Glass Jug. Body in dark brown,
speckled with splashes of white.
(*Loco Antiques*)

Flask in Nailsea Glass. Main body in clear
glass, decorated with white loopings.
(*Loco Antiques*)

rainbow. Cut glass has a very satisfying feel, its precise, sharp, clean outer faces are pleasant to handle.

The cuts in glass were made with discs of polished slate, and fine sandstone. Cast iron discs were also used in conjunction with a cutting medium of sand and water. After cutting, the surfaces were polished with discs made of cast tin, copper, and even wood and cork, in conjunction with very fine abrasives such as jewellers rouge, and special putty made with calcined tin.

Glass cutting was a decoration that was not necessarily undertaken by the glass makers, in fact, in the early 19th century, there were many works specialising in cutting only. Glass merchants would buy the undecorated glass blanks for cutters in their employ to finish.

The quality of glass up to the mid 18th century, in

respect of refractiveness, was not particularly good, it possessed a cloudyness that prevented good transmission of light rays, consequently cutting was limited to shallow faceting and scalloping, but from the late 18th century, when crystal clear flint glass was available, the cutting became more elaborate.

Designs were also added to glass by engraving. This was accomplished by scratching the glass with a diamond or by " pricking " tiny dots to form a pattern. Etching was a quick and relatively cheap process for decorating glass, using hydrofluoric acid as an etching agent. The articles were treated with an acid resistant varnish and the design scratched on it to expose the glass. It was subsequently immersed in acid, which bit the pattern into the surface.

Roman and Syrian glass is not for the collector, these are mainly museum pieces. Neither is he likely to obtain any medieval European or Islamic glass, these periods are far too early for a new collector, even if he had the opportunity to add such fantastically rare pieces to a possible collection.

One could not do better than start with English glass from about 1820 to 1900, this is virtually Victorian glass although it is appreciated that if we are to be particularly precise that Victoria was born in 1837 and died in 1901. One of the most interesting fields of Victorian glass is Nailsea. Nailsea glass is usually characterised by a greenish bottle glass in which flecks of other colours, including white, has been skilfully amalgamated.

It is interesting to note that taxes influenced the early glass industrialist, green glass, which was normally glass in its natural colour, was taxed, but at a lesser rate than clear glass which had been rendered colourless.

Nailsea, from which this particular glass obtains its name, is a town near Bristol where John Robert Lucas started his glass house in 1788, but Nailsea glass was not the exclusive product of John Robert Lucas, it is known that it was produced at Wrockwardine in Shropshire,

Warrington, Sunderland, Newcastle, Stourbridge and Alloa in Scotland and probably elsewhere.

The examples produced by these various glass houses are so similar that it is difficult to ascertain their precise origin, therefore, Nailsea will be considered as a general group.

The earliest Nailsea was a brownish green bottle glass decorated with lines of white enamel, and either mottled or flecked. It is estimated that this was produced between about 1790 and 1820. Between 1800 and 1820 the bottle glass became a light green in colour and decorated with notched ornamentation. From about 1815 opaque coloured glass was introduced with mottled and looped decoration, flecking was also included with this type of bottle. Up to 1845, crossing and interlacing strips of opaque and clear glass was used to decorate a pale green bottle, this was followed by the same ornamentation on clear flint glass. From about 1845 coloured flint glass was introduced decorated with contrasting tints.

From the foregoing it will be obvious that we have five broad groups in which to classify our Nailsea glass and some rough indication of date. One of the most attractive decorations used on this type of ware is known as Looping or Dragging. It is a familiar decoration on iced cakes, threads of contrasting colour are added to the body and then dragged upwards by a pointed tool to form reasonably precise wavy bands around the vessel. This form of decoration has been used since ancient times.

The flecks which appear in Nailsea are usually white or bluish white in colour and feel slightly rough when touched with the finger. The speckles may be so dense that they cover the bottle completely or in other instances will be sprinkled thinly. Yellow and red speckles occur occasionally and are eagerly sought by the collector.

Gimmels are not a modern invention, quite attractive examples were produced in Nailsea. A gimmel is the two flask container that is used today for oil and vinegar. The two bottles were blown separately and then fused together, their necks curved so that they are pointing in opposite directions. The Nailsea gimmel was usually produced with pink and white spiral decorations, or with white crossing and interlacing strips of opaque glass.

Nailsea candlesticks were shaped from short lengths of glass tube. One end was formed into a down spreading foot with a folded rim, the socket was also enlarged with a thick rim and ornamented, the smallest was about 6″ high and the tallest approximately one foot.

The following items are just a few of the forms of Nailsea glass that the collector can seek.

Flasks made in the form of hand bellows often used for perfumes, Jacobs ladders, glass bells, coaching horns, shepherds crooks, glass masses, riding crops, tobacco pipes, walking sticks, canes and the yard of ale.

The yard of ale was of course a trick glass, it measured approximately 3ft. in length and usually terminated in a hollow bulb. The theory behind the yard of ale is that once it had been filled it cannot be stood upright because of its rounded end, consequently the drinker has to drain it to the bitter end. When the vessel is raised about the shoulder of the consumer during the act of drinking, the liquid in the hollow bulb suddenly drains down inside of the long glass into the face of the user.

The more useful examples include very attractive jugs, flasks, perhaps with a pewter cap, serving bottles, tumblers, rolling pins, jars and mugs.

Before leaving Nailsea a word about friggers. This was a term used to describe unofficial pieces of work, these were executed by workmen or apprentices for their own amusement, pleasure and perhaps profit. The work of friggers is generally included in with that of Nailsea. Articles commonly frigged are rolling pins, which were often painted in oil colours with inscriptions and scenes.

Very elaborate ornaments were produced by friggers including fully rigged ships, sometimes complete with crew members, and fox hunting scenes with hounds.

It is not thought that the general quantity of glass ware produced by friggers is very great, and it is only mentioned here as a matter of interest to the collector.

The Victorian era saw the birth of slag glass, which has the appearance of marble. It is opaque, mottled, and complete with veining. It is also known as purple slag or marble glass and as " end of day wear ". Two of the many better known makers of the glass were J. G. Sowerby of Gateshead and Thornhill Leas near Wakefield, Yorkshire.

Slag, the waste material which floats on the top of molten steel in blast furnaces, was skimmed off and used by the glass makers for mixing with clear glass, other materials such as sand and colouring were added, depending upon the ultimate requirement of the glass. It may appear that the manufacture of slag was a slap happy operation, but, in fact, the whole operation was skilfully conducted.

The name " end of day wear " referred to the operators in the blast furnace rather than the glass makers. The slag was drawn off shortly before the steel was tapped at the end of the puddlers day.

J. G. Sowerby in the late 1860's was producing slag glass pieces in beautiful variegated colours, opals, blue and green mixtures, and turquoises.

The Victorians used a wide variety of coloured glass, and were very experimental in its use. The collector will find many items to interest him made from slag glass. All the usual paraphernalia of useful and not very useful articles can be collected. Some of the minor items will include salt cellars, and comport, tumblers, pin trays, spill holders, pilgrim bottle vases, vases of many designs and shapes, dishes and plates.

The Bristol blue glass of the early Victorian period was a near royal blue known as Kings Blue. The name Kings Blue originated after George IV had expressed his delight and admiration of a spirit set presented to him as a coronation gift in 1821. This costly royal blue glass was produced until 1840, but due to refining treatments given to the cobalt oxide which removed important minerals, the colouring qualities deteriorated.

Collectors of Bristol blue glass will certainly want to collect earlier pieces than Victorian, collectors usually prefer 18th century tableware. Unfortunately the name Bristol blue has become less specific and is now used to describe any dark blue or translucent glass.

The term Bristol Blue did not necessarily originate to indicate where the glass was made. Bristol was the only place where the smalt, which is used to colour the glass, could be obtained, and what is more surprising, there was only one merchant stocking it!

Smalt is a vitreous form of cobalt oxide and is used for colouring glass blue.

Opaque—white or enamel glass, which is now generally described as " South Staffordshire ", was made in England from about the mid 18th century. It is a material that closely approximates porcelain, and may well have been invented as a cheaper alternative to that material.

Enamel glass has little resistance to heat, therefore it was not used very extensively for domestic articles normally subjected to relatively high temperatures; when such articles were occasionally made, they were invariably robust in section.

The dense whiteness of the glass was obtained by the addition of tin oxide to flint glass. The addition of this chemical, however, made the material somewhat brittle, and although doubly annealed this brittle property was never completely eradicated. Articles made in enamel glass have a smooth texture, but it is a relatively soft material that scratches easily, the scratches showing dark as they become grimed with dirt. If examined up to a light the material will be found to have a creamy translucence.

Pieces of opaque-white glassware are often decorated with designs and patterns, not necessarily executed by the original manufacturer. Anyone so inclined could buy plain white specimens and add the decorations to suit themselves.

Early decorated examples using unfired pigments and colours, and gilded motifs, lacked the resistance of fired enamels, and with constant handling and the passage of time, they have either become obliterated, or completely worn away. The decorative work was applied with oil colours, enamels requiring heat firing, and oil gilding which was a low temperature process.

Another method employed from about 1760 by Sadler and Green to embellish was by the use of a black transfer print, which was subsequently overpainted with enamel colours.

Many interesting examples of this glass can be collected including chemists' jars, often labelled in gold, snuff boxes, bodkin cases, wine bottles, scent phials, tea caddies, jugs, mugs, flower bowls, vases, candlesticks, tapesticks, cruet stands, and almost every type of holloware normally found in porcelain.

An interesting development in glass was furthered in England by Apsley Pellatt, who was the proprietor of the Falcon glass works in Southwark. Originally a French invention, the technique involved embedding small models of a ceramic material in clear glass.

The models of portraits, flowers and other subjects were formed from a ceramic paste which had two important properties—it did not form gas when heated and its rates of expansion and contraction were very similar to those of glass into which it was to be sealed.

This was obviously important if the two materials were not to fracture on cooling.

This type of glassware is known as Sulphides, Cameo Incrustations, and Crystallo-Ceramics.

The first of the Crystallo-Ceramics was produced by Pellatt in England about 1820 and continued in production until about 1850, but he was not the only source, other English manufacturers continued after this date, and of course, the French were producing during the same period.

Paperweights, tankards, candelabra, scent bottles,

Goblet and wine glass with engraved decoration. Late 18th-early 19th century.

(Victoria and Albert Museum, Crown copyright)

pendants, small bottles and aromatic vinegar bottles, are just a few of the articles treated by this process.

Wine glasses provide an excellent medium for the collector, offering as they do, a fascinating subject for study, especially if the collector is interested in having pieces to show the development of the wine glass. More modest collections can, of course, be formed by limiting the range to periods, types, or styles. The development of wine glass stems was briefly as follows:—

1680 to 1710. Inverted Baluster. Period when glasses were adapted from the Venetians bowls. " V " shaped with wide mouths, very robust designs. Stem bellied, one side tapering, the other side rounded at top.

1690 to 1710. Drop Knop. Stem with urn shaped bulge just below the bowl to prevent glass slipping through fingers.

1695 to 1715. Angular Knop. Flattened knop, horizontally positioned. Air bubbles or " tears " introduced as a stem decoration.
Ball Knop. Bulge in stem spherical like a glass marble, often placed immediately above a shoulder.

1695 to 1725. Annulated or Triple-ring Knop. Stem with flattened rings, triple-ringed, usually one ring in between two others in close proximity.

1700 to 1720. Multiple Knops. Knops of similar shape repeated.

1710 to 1730. True Baluster. Knop with bellied, rounded base, tapering into the stem above.

1710 to 1715. Acorn Knop. A tooled design in the form of an acorn, sometimes inverted.
Mushroom Knop. Shaped like a mushroom, curved on top, with an acute return to the stem below.

1715 to 1730. Silesian Stem. Moulded pedestal.

The above are general descriptions of stem types, together with an indication of their periods, but do not be surprised to find a stem that does not specifically fit any of these categories. There was no requirement for the manufacturers to follow any specification. Fashion and the necessity to sell their products, together with the individual ideas of the manufacturers, often influenced the finished article.

Tears were added to stems by a simple process. The glass was indented and covered with more molten glass. The air trapped in the indentation, expanded by the heat, formed a bubble, which was elongated during the process of drawing the stem.

The base, or foot, of wine glasses up to 1750 had a folded edge. This was effected by turning the rim back under the base and folding flat, and so provided a much strengthened rim, which was less prone to damage. Later examples do not have this feature.

Bowl shapes also varied considerably in size and shape, depending upon the liquid they were intended to contain. From the early conical bowl with hardly any stem, they employed other shapes known as bucket, round funnel, flanged, cup or ovid, ogee, trumpet, and bell shaped.

Decorations include cutting, elongated air bubbles in stems (air twist), twisted stems, coloured glass and coloured twists and engraving.

GLOSSARY

Ale Glass: A long narrow glass for serving ale.

Air Twist: Mostly found in drinking vessels, and shafts of candlesticks. Tube-like veins produced by drawing an entrapped air bubble.

Amberina: An amber glass mixture containing gold. Colour ranges yellow to dark red.

Anglo-Venetian Glass: Glassware made of soda-glass in London from about 1570 until about 1680.

Annealing: Process of relieving stresses in glass by re-heating and permitting the glass to cool slowly.

Arabesques: Scroll works, engraved on hollow-ware of flowers and leaves.

Aventurine: Originally discovered by accident in Murano, Italy, copper crystals were added to the melt which resulted in a dark brown glass, gold flecked.

Baluster: This refers to the shape seen in a balustrade, the graceful swelling central curve also used to decorate the stems of drinking vessels, and candlesticks.

Blow Moulding: Detailed in text.

Broken-Swirl: A double moulding process. The glass is first moulded with vertical ribs, removed from the mould and twisted. It is then returned to the mould and vertical rib re-impressed over the swirls.

Calcedonia: A type of glass, the colour and veining similar to chalcedony, first produced in 15th century.

Cane: Rods of coloured glass used as inserts for obtaining coloured streaks and forming patterns in paperweights.

Cased Glass: One layer of glass over another, of a different colour.

Compote: Bowl mounted on a foot.

Cresting: A fluted fillet used to join the stem of a glass to the bowl. Can be small or extended half way up the bowl.

Crimping: Dents, or flutes formed by a tool used on a foot or handle.

Cristal: A term used to describe fine table and decorative glass of all kinds.

Crown Glass: Early form of glass used for windows.

Crystal: A term used to describe the best quality clear flint glass.

Cullet: Clean broken glass melted into new mixtures of glass.

Cutting: Detailed in text.

Cyst: A circular protuberance usually found in the lower part of a wine glass bowl.

Dram Glasses: Other names include Joeys, Nips, Gin Glasses, and Genettes. Small glasses for spirits.

Etched Glass. Detailed in text.

Filigree Glass: A decoration involving interwoven spirals of white and coloured glass threads.

Finials: A knob, usually added to covers.

Firing Glasses: A strong, stumpy glass with thick stem and a flat foot. Also known as hammering glasses, because they were used to bang the table to show appreciation, much the same as present day hand clapping.

Flashed Glass: A coating of coloured glass over clear.

Flint Glass: This glass was developed by George Ravenscroft (1618–81) in England. The silica, which occurs in nature in most rocks was obtained from calcined flints. Hollow-ware made from flint glass has a decided ring when flicked with finger nails, and has a better refractive quality than any glass made up to this period.

Flute: A deep, conical bowled drinking glass, or a vertical cut or cuts, i.e. fluting.

Free Blown: Method of blowing glass without the aid of moulds, relying entirely on the skill of the glass blower. (See text.)

Green Glass: Glass in its natural colour.

Kick: Cone shaped indentation found in the base of early bottles and decanters.

Latticinio: Filigree glass made by interlacing strips of clear and opaque glass. Originally a Venetian development.

Lattimo: White glass made with lead, Early 16th century; made at Murano, Italy.

Lead Glass: Glass in which lead oxide was used as a fluxing agent. See " Flint Glass ".

Merese: A connecting piece of glass, used to join a bowl and stem, shaped like a button or simply a wafer of glass.

Mould Blown: Detailed in text.

Picot: Tooled decoration, an edging.

Pomona Glass: A stippled effect obtained by the use of acid. Unstippled portions of the glass were stained a yellowish-straw colour.

Pressed Glass: Detailed in text.

Prunts: Moulded or tooled pieces of decoration that are applied as a separate part of the body of the article during its manufacture.

Punties: Concave cuts in paperweights.

Quilling: Quill-like also known as pinched trailing. A strip of glass is added and pinched to form repetitive pleats.

Reticello: Lace glass. A decoration with a net-work of white opaque threads beneath the surface. First produced in Venice about 15th century.

Reticulated: A pattern similar to netting, diamond like formations of crazing.

Rigaree Marks: Produced by a small metal wheel, its tiny contiguous ribs produced by bands of glass tooled in vertical lines.

Romer: A drinking vessel of pale green glass, similar to a wine glass but bowl spherical, and stem and foot hollow, freely decorated with prunts.

Rummer: Short stemmed drinking glass.

Scalloping: A decorative shape like the end of a scallop shell, usually used on rims or series of semi circles.

Seeds: Tiny air bubbles trapped in the glass, usually caused by an insufficiently heated furnace, which otherwise would drive the air out completely.

Spangled Glass: Decoration obtained by rolling molten glass over particles of metal or flakes of mica. Subsequently fused by heating.

String Rim: The raised band around the top of the neck of a bottle, for securing string or wire to retain the stopper or cork.

Sulphides: Detailed in text.

Swirl: Radiating spirally, as formed in paperweights by canes of various colours.

Swirled Ribbing: A decoration formed by twisting a stem or similar shape that has been previously ribbed vertically.

Tale Glass: A second quality glass taken from the top of the pot, the glass taken from the bottom of the pots is much finer.

Threading or Thread Circuit: A thin thread of glass continuously wound around the rim of a bowl or neck of a vessel.

Three-piece glasses: Glasses in which the bowl, stem, and foot have been made separately.

Toddy Lifter: A type of pipette tube for lifting hot toddy from bowl to glass.

Trailed ornament: Looping threads of glass added to a bowl or foot.

Two-piece Glasses: Glasses made by drawing the stem from the bowl. The foot is then added as a separate piece.

Venetian Glass: This is a soda glass, blown thinly, and worked at relatively low temperatures and required great speed in working.

Vermicular Collar: A trace of glass surround a decanter neck or stem, formed into a wave.

Writhing: Swirling ribbing, surface twisting, on bowl or stem.

IVORY AND BONE

Ivory as a basic carving material has been used since primitive times. From the days of the Romans it has been used continually for personal adornment, statues, inlays, and for thousands of other purposes. The study of ivory could provide a continuous record of man's tastes and fashions through this extensive period.

The best ivory comes from the tusks of African elephants and the quality of wild elephant ivory is much superior to that taken from captive animals.

The largest tusks recorded from an African elephant is eleven and a half feet, and the combined weight of both tusks was 293 pounds! The sole source of ivory is the elephant's tusk, but other bones have been used, and these are often difficult to distinguish from the real thing. These alternatives include fossilised tusks of mammoths, rhinoceros horn, walrus and narwhal tusks.

The majority of ivory carvings are small, mainly because the raw material is limited in size, but it is an ideal substance for carving and lends itself readily to details of a delicate nature. It also has a warm smooth feel, which softly mellows with age, and it takes a lightly polished finish very readily.

How does one start to collect ivory, when the subjects available are so enormous? Personally if the specimen is ivory, attractive, and the price is not above my means, I would need no other incentive—I would buy it, and be happy that I had acquired another piece of ivory.

However, the choice is a personal one, and the collector may wish to specialise with figures, netsuké, bodkin cases and small boxes, cane handles, novelties, or some other subject of his own choice. The following descriptions of various pieces may help in that choice.

Balls within a Ball

Everyone must, at some time, have seen examples of this oriental novelty in ivory, consisting of an outer ball with a number of diminishing size balls trapped within. Each ball is separate and can move freely within the con-

Miniature ivory elephants on wooden pedestal.
(*D. C. Gohm*)

fines of the ball encompassing it. All of the balls are usually beautifully carved.

The balls-in-a ball have a long history in the East, and no doubt, they are still being produced there.

The method used to achieve this apparent impossibility was first to make the ivory into a sphere or ball, and then drill holes to a certain depth in positions dictated by the requirements of final design. Then with a sharp carving tool, the interstices between the drilled holes were cut away to release a ball, repeated cutting away through another layer released the second ball, and so on until all the balls were free. The decorative carving was executed during this process.

These novelties are also known as Devils Balls, and are often a feature of chessmen of Eastern origin.

Eight Immortals

The eight immortals are a collection of Chinese figures, roughly synonymous with the Catholic saints. They have been represented in many media, including porcelain, but, in my opinion, the ivory examples are the best.

They are representative of masculinity, femininity, wealth, poverty, youth, age, aristocracy, and plebeianism, though not necessarily in that order: and they are indicative of the Taoist principles that censure the worship of power and material things.

The little figures are named and recognition features have been added.

Chung-Li-Ch'uan.	Usually carries a fan.
Ho Hsien-ku.	A figure of a woman, usually with flowers, lotus bloom, or ladle.
Lu Tung-pin.	Cap pleated and carries a sword.
Li Ti'eh-kua.	A really ugly fellow with crutch.
Chang Kuo-hao.	Bearded face, carries a drum.
Ts'ao Kuo-chiu.	Bearded, carries tickets.
Lan Ts'ai-ho.	Carries flowers either in a basket or as a bouquet.
Han Hsiang-tzu.	Carries a broken branch.

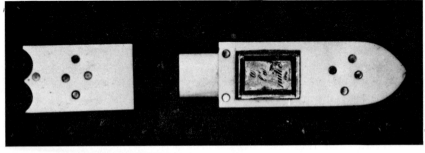

Ivory Bodkin Case, engraved "a l'amitie" (for friendship).
(*Aldate Ltd.*)

Snuff Rasps

Snuff rasps made and used during the 17th century, for grating tobacco into snuff. They consisted of a section of ivory about 2 inches wide and 6 to 7 inches long. The back was carved with groups of figures, or made in the form of a single figure, the front carried perforated iron grates.

The majority of snuff grates were produced in Dieppe, but they were also made in the Low countries, Germany and England.

Crucifixes

17th century crucifixes were often carved from a single piece of ivory, including the body of Christ. It was also a practice of this period to produce the body of Christ in ivory, and mount it on a wooden cross. These were of European origin.

BONE

Bone carvings are closely allied to those of ivory, as a raw material they both come from animal "bone", and sometimes it may be difficult for the layman to differentiate between the two. There is, however, a considerable difference in the cost and availability of each material. Bone may lack the quality of ivory but objects made in this material are very collectable.

We can thank the French prisoners captured during the Napoleonic wars for some very beautiful work in bone. During these wars, which covered a period from 1793 to 1815, it is estimated that over 60,000 prisoners were housed in this country, either in prisons or in prison ships. Like any army, there were all types and trades represented in their number, including ivory and jet carvers.

As a means of obtaining money for a few luxuries, and as a means to pass away the time, these craftsmen manufactured articles which could be sold to visitors to the prison on open days. Surprisingly, the prisoners were allowed and even encouraged to market their products. Some prisons allowed visitors to call once or twice a week especially to trade and to bring raw materials. The raw materials were probably more necessary for the other trades being carried on than for the bone carvers who had their own way of obtaining materials. They collected the bones from their own meat rations and buried them for a period to get them clean. They were then subsequently split into convenient pieces for carving or for model making.

When the project got under way it was common practice for the prisoners to form groups, each man specialising in a particular part of the model or carving in current production.

Model Ships

The ship models produced by prisoners of war were very fine examples indeed. They were produced in exquisite detail and as accurate as they could be made under the conditions. Remember the prisoners had no drawings from which they could work, so they were compelled to rely on their memory.

Games

Bone chess pieces, playing cards, draughts and dominoes, were all made by the prisoners, initially no doubt as a pastime and as a means of providing games for their own amusement.

Later these games were packaged in suitable bone boxes and sold in considerable numbers. Some of the boxes were quite elaborate with sliding lids, and decorated with water colour paintings.

Playing cards were often quite tiny rectangles of bone with the symbols added in oil paint.

The French prisoners of war were not the only source of bone carving. Many small and interesting pieces originated from other sources, like the pocket domino set illustrated. This is a Victorian novelty for carrying in the pocket. The dominoes are quite roughly finished, but the little brass box, leather covered, is beautifully made with a hinged lid with an inserted bevelled glass window.

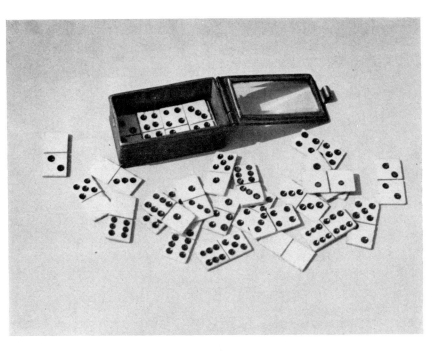

Miniature pocket set of Victorian dominoes in bone, case with bevelled
glass lid, and leather bound sides.
(*D. C. Gohm*)

Guillotine Models

These gruesome models were made with the same
care and attention to detail that is typical of prisoner-of-
war work. The models were made in various sizes, and a
few even had a model figure, with hands tied behind his
back, in the process of being executed. To add to the
effect, decapitated heads with bloody necks, were placed
in the basket under the blade. " Blood " was added
beneath the blade to complete the realism.

Mechanical Toys

Mechanical toys, with limited motions, were made to
operate by a series of ratchets and wheels made from
bone. Threads connected to the wheels and the operating
handle completed the mechanism. Spindles, etc., required
for their production, may have been supplied by a local

turner, if not, it would not have been beyond the wit of such talented craftsmen to have devised a simple lathe for themselves.

Toys with mechanical motions include women spinning, nursing babies, and soldiers.

Cribbage Boards

Apart from the standard bone cribbage board, these were also made in a box form with a sliding lid, with glass let into the sides, under which were set small watercolour paintings.

Other Examples

These include clock-cases, domino-boxes, fans, mirror-frames, seals, chessmen, playing cards, miniature toys, watch-cases, lace-bobbins, thimbles, needle-cases, etc.

MAPS AND CHARTS

In this day and age it would be impossible to take an antique map and navigate oneself from one town to another.

Early maps did not contain the refinement of roads, but what they lacked in detail they certainly made up for in charm, and decoration. Collecting old maps and charts can be considered an extension of print collecting, it does form an automatic specialisation forming a category in its own right.

Good quality maps are almost as rare as good quality prints, but they *are* obtainable and if one starts with lesser known map makers they can be bought for a few pounds. The vast majority of antique maps and charts were straightforward engravings on copper, and with the most attractive, the cartography is by no means the most important factor from the collector's point of view. Decorations in the form of cartouches, inset pictures of towns, villages, and places of interest, or perhaps charts with dolphins playing in the seas, and cherubs blowing winds into the bellowing sails of galleons, turns a map or chart into a colourful work more prized for the artistry than for the topographical details portrayed.

Charles Bickham (1743–96) drew early charming birds eye views of English Counties for " British Monarchy " between the years 1750 and 1754. Although not maps in the strictly technical sense, they are interesting nevertheless, the counties being shown as if seen from a balloon.

Michael Drayton (1612–22) included in his maps figures dotted about the countryside, including shepherdesses, Goddesses, nymphs and animals.

During the latter half of the 17th century John Ogilby produced the forerunner of the route map. These beautifully executed maps were drawn in the form of a continuous scroll, the route shown clearly, with information that would permit the traveller to find his bearings. When going up hill, a small hill was shown with the route climbing up the side, a down hill path was shown by placing the hill upside down on the map. Each strip of the scroll was orientated by a compass indicating North. The large cartouche placed in the centre of the top edge usually shows a scene, and details of the general route.

Of all the Cartographers I much prefer the work of Jan Jansson and John Speed. The work of these two map makers was very fine indeed. Large and elegant cartouches abounded together with colourful coats of arms. John Speed and a few others indicated the colours to be used when painting the heraldic motives. O = Or (Gold), A = Argent (Silver or White), G = Gules (Red), S = Sable (Black) and so on.

Christopher Saxton, in the 16th century, made the most complete survey of the country taken up to that time. Such was the importance of this work that the Privy Council issued an order that assistance should be given him on demand to help with this undertaking.

When buying Saxton county maps or any relatively expensive map, obtain them from a reputable dealer until sufficient knowledge has been gained to assess them for yourself.

Many impressions were taken from Saxton plates over a number of years. With changes in paper and the loss of definition through wear of the plates, the value of the map could be well below the price asked.

Because of the high demand for attractive maps such as those produced by Jansson and Speed, modern reprints are infiltrating the market. These cheap reproductions are suitable as decorative pieces for non-collectors. However they will not stand comparison with a genuine old map with its indefinable quality of paper and print.

The majority of maps by John Speed were produced as an atlas, and each map carries a list of the hundreds and some information about the county on the back. When framing this type of map, use glass for both the front and back so that this information can still be read.

MAPMAKERS

1574–9	Christopher Saxton.	English and Welsh County Maps.
1599–1676	Pieter van de Keere.	Miniature County Maps.
1607–37	William Camden.	County Maps.
1611–1670	John Speed.	County Maps of England and Wales. Map of Scotland and Ireland.
1612–22	Michael Drayton.	Imaginative Maps of England and Wales.
1626	John Bill.	Miniature County Maps.
1635–36	Mathew Simons.	Tiny County Maps.
1643	Thomas Jenner.	Tiny County Maps.
1645	John Blaeu.	County Maps of England, Wales and Scotland. Maps of Ireland.
1645	Jan Jansson.	County Maps of England and Wales. Maps of Scotland and Ireland.
1671–73	Richard Blome.	County Maps.
1695–1773	John Sellar.	County Maps small.
1675–1698	John Ogilby.	Road Maps (England & Wales).
1690	Philip Lea.	Saxton Maps reprints with additions.
1695–1772	Robert Morden.	County Maps.
1715–16	Thomas Taylor.	County Maps.
1719	Thomas Gardner.	Road Maps.
1720–1764	Owen & Bowen.	Small County Maps of England and Wales.

1724	Herman Moll.	County Maps of England, Wales, Scotland and Ireland.
1742–45	Thomas Badeslade.	County Maps of England.
1743–96	George Bickham.	Aerial View of Counties
1744–45	Dodsley & Cowley.	County Maps of England and Wales.
1746	Samuel Simpson.	County Maps of England.
1746	John Rocque.	County Maps of England and Wales.
1747–60	Thomas Kitchen.	English County Maps.
1748–50	T. Osbourne.	English County Maps.
1749–55	Emanuel Bowen. Thomas Kitchen.	Large County Maps.
1766	John Ellis.	County Maps.
1785	Carington Bowles.	County Maps.
1787–1831	John Cary.	County Maps.
1836	Thomas Moule.	County Maps of England.

NETSUKÉ AND INRO

The national costumes of Japan, unlike European dress, made no provision for carrying the paraphernalia of everyday life. The kimonos were buttonless gowns; and those worn by the males were supported by a wide sash. As the costumes were pocketless, personal articles were secured to the person by means of a netsuké. A netsuké is in effect a decorative toggle, attached to a cord; the other end of the cord carried such personal articles as a tobacco pouch, sweet meat box, snuff bottle, and a small container for carrying a seal and red pigment, medicines, and herbs. Such items are termed an Inro.

The assembly of netsuké, cord, and inro were attached to the person by passing the cord behind the sash so that the netsuké rested on the top edge, thus preventing the cord from slipping.

Generally a netsuké was designed compactly without any projections which would catch in the costume material, and the backs were flattened so that they would fit comfortably against the body. Card holes, usually two in number, are often joined by a channel to hold the cord. Older netsuké often had one hole larger than the other to receive the cord knot.

A netsuké is usually made of wood or ivory, and is frequently found in the human or animal form, but they were also carved to represent many other forms, including reptiles, birds, fruits, insects, zodiac animals, legendary figures and even household utensils.

The Japanese zodiac animals were the rat, ox, tiger, hare, dragon, serpent, horse, goat, monkey, cock, dog and boar. Each animal represented a two hour period of the day and night, for example 10 p.m. until midnight was the " hour " of the boar.

Netsuké first made its appearance about 1780, although they were produced as early as the 15th century. They were not considered to be of any real value and consequently they were discarded when they became damaged. From 1780 to about 1870 was their best period, many fine pieces were carved, and even carried the signature or initials of the artist. From 1870 onwards, there was a general decline in their use.

Shibayama is a name given to a particular method of inlaying metals and mother-of-pearl into the ivories. This

Netsuké. 26 different types.
(*Victoria and Albert Museum, Crown copyright*)

type of netsuké was very skilfully executed and makes a most desirable possession.

When buying netsuké again use your judgement, look for detail and the obvious skill of the craftsman. Make certain that no part is damaged or broken.

Ivory netsuké may be cleaned with a very soft brush or hand polished but remember they can suffer from excessive heat and light.

PAPERWEIGHTS IN GLASS

The glass paperweights known as Millefiore, meaning "thousand flowers", offers the collector a rare opportunity to acquire items that were made over a very limited period.

Undoubtedly the best period was between 1845 and 1849, but if the collector restricts himself to these dates his collection will remain very small indeed, unless he is a man of considerable means. It is suggested that he extends the period from 1845 to about 1880, and so provide an opportunity of buying much cheaper. Fine quality, early paperweights made about the middle of the 19th century can command very high prices. In 1965, at a London saleroom, one such piece was sold for £3,000!

The best early pieces were French, and came from factories in Clichy, Baccarat, and St. Louis, but other countries, including England and America, produced excellent specimens. The glass paperweights were shown at The Great Exhibition of 1851, but they did not seem to become very popular until sometime later when it was realised that they were indeed small works of art in their own right.

Another type of paperweight than can usually be bought reasonably is the domed or raised block of glass which acts as a magnifying glass and has a coloured print stuck to the underside, showing views of towns, holiday resorts, places of interest, street scenes, and foreign views. There is a considerable range of subjects from which to choose.

It is known that this type of paperweight existed in about 1851, and probably dates from that period, i.e. later 19th century. As time progressed, the coloured print was superseded by the photographic print, but these lack the colour and appeal of their predecessors.

Prior to 1870, the weights were usually circular, but following this period, they became more elaborate and were produced in the shape of horseshoes, hearts, and other decorative outlines.

Millefiori paperweight.
(*Loco Antiques*)

The outlet for this type of paperweight was mainly through stationers, and apart from their practical use, had a souvenir value, therefore it may be possible to start your collection whilst on holiday, or visiting a town on business. Antique shops in these areas are more likely to show interest in such items than those in the London area.

Apsley Pellatt was an English manufacturer of note, he made paperweights with a small slab or plaque of white china with the design shown in relief. This was then embedded in glass. (See Glass Crystallo Ceramie.)

A millefiore paperweight is a crystal ball (not unlike the crystal used by fortune tellers) with a galaxy of brightly coloured flowers imprisoned in its body. Instead of flowers, one might find reptiles, salamanders, snakes, and butterflies, or even portraits.

You have probably seen hundreds of modern copies of the famous millefiore in gift and antique shops, but these are not valuable and do not warrant a place in your collection. It is easy to select the real specimen by the overall quality of workmanship after only a little practical experience.

The base of a glass paperweight may have an un-finished spot, called " a pontil-mark ". This was caused when the glass was broken off the pontil rod by the glass worker at the completion of the manufacturing cycle, and can be taken as an indication that the piece is old.

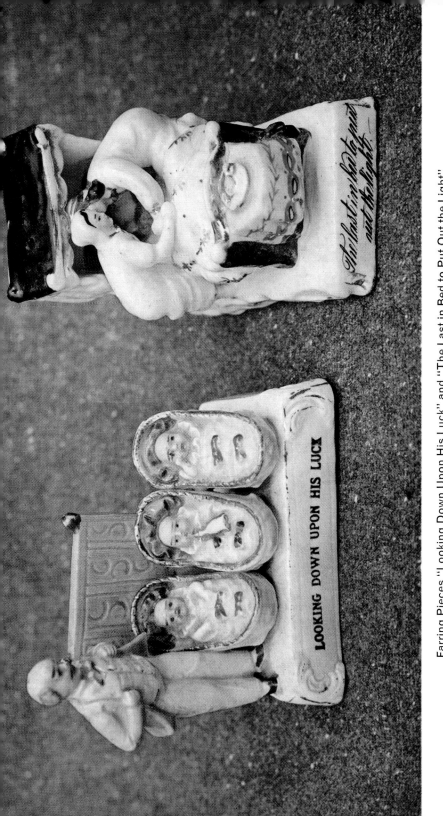

Fairing Pieces "Looking Down Upon His Luck" and "The Last in Bed to Put Out the Light".

Part of Minton Dinner Service with "Byzantine", design, Registry mark dated 6th October, 1870

PAINTINGS AND PICTURES

The art of painting, in its many forms, has been practiced by man since he emerged from pre-history, and it is one of the oldest art forms. What other art form could go back 20,000 years to the caves of Altamira, and provide such wonderful examples.

How then, can a subject so vast, and covering such a long period, be adequately covered in a few thousand words? Obviously it cannot, therefore in keeping with the aim of this book, we will make the introduction, guide the reader through the preliminaries to whet his appetite, and then leave him to pursue the path of his choice.

Do not be dismayed by the high prices being paid for old Masters, these prices do not necessarily reflect the true value, which after all, is arbitrary. There are plenty of excellent pictures that can be bought without mortgaging your house, and if you use your judgement, they will certainly increase in value, and give many hours of pleasant contemplation.

The opportunity of discovering an exceptional oil painting is unlikely to say the least, but oil paintings, like every other commodity, are governed by supply and demand, and of course, fashion. Step outside the fashion and you will find excellent works, either by minor artists, or by lesser known ones, relatively cheaply. If you are fortunate in anticipating the likely demands for fashion during the next few years, who knows what price your painting would command?

Oil paintings have been executed on wooden panels, copper, tin, stretched canvas, and many other supports. All of these are acceptable, and in general terms, do not affect the cost or desirability. Large paintings are invariably on canvas for convenience of the artist.

Catalogues will often refer to a painting as—Italian School, or English School. School in this sense is a term used to state that the painting originated in that country, and that usually the artist is unknown. School is sometimes used in another sense—such as School of Rembrandt—meaning that it has all the characteristics of a Rembrandt painting, but was not executed by him. It may have been the work of assistants, or copyists.

Brushwork is another important consideration to the expert. The bristles of the brush, charged with paint and applied over canvas, are as individual as an artist's handwriting. Experts familiar with the works of a particular artist, can recognise his work simply from the brushwork.

Paintings described as " conversation pieces " are not as may be expected groups of people having a chat, but a special kind of painting showing two or more portraits in surrounding scenery, usually appropriate to the subject.

Icons originally referred to a picture of Christ, or a Saint on a separate panel, to distinguish the work from those executed on walls. These are often turning up in sale rooms, usually in most elaborate frames.

An interesting technique of painting is known as " optical mixtures ". The object of this technique is to obtain brighter secondary colours by placing primary colours in close proximity, in tiny blobs, so that the eye mixes the colours when viewed from a distance. For example, blue and yellow blobs of paint would appear green.

The word " primitive " is often applied to paintings of a particular style or date. It sounds informed if the description is used among uninformed circles, but the word is practically meaningless now, except for giving an undeserved importance to the work of amateur artists whose only claim to fame is their lack of technical skill and vision, which is obvious in their childlike daubings.

Size of pictures will be an important consideration for the collector. Very large pictures will require the space to hang them, and with present day houses, this is not always available, consequently the smaller and more manageable pictures are those usually desired. This has an effect on the cost. Excellent quality, large sized, pictures will often be cheaper than the poorer quality smaller varieties.

Before buying your first oil painting, get to know your own taste. This is not to suggest that a collector does not know the subjects that excites him most, but oil paintings have a tendency to " grow on you " and pictures turned down with a cursory examination will often become enchanting with longer association. Conversely the opposite can happen. Some art galleries, specialising in " minor masters " will often be pleased to loan a picture on approval, so that the collector has the opportunity to see it in his own home, and " get to know it " before making his final decision.

Do not bother to acquire paintings in very bad condition, just because they are cheap, unless of course you suspect you have found an old masterpiece. The cost of restoring will often outweigh any original advantage in price, and extensive restoring is unsatisfactory.

Still life paintings, which reached their zenith during the seventeeth and early eighteenth century, are not avidly sought after today. I can only assume the lack of action usually projected by such pictures is not in keeping with the modern mood. This is a great shame, many still life subjects are beautiful compositions of natural objects, re-arranged for the sake of design, colour, and lighting.

Flower pieces, often executed with great attention to detail, are much in demand as decorative furnishing pieces, and consequently many cost a little more than still life subjects.

Shipping paintings are in high demand, and if the quality is in any way acceptable, prices will be high.

Water-colour painting is an art that has been particularly exploited by English artists, and these are the finest in the world. True water-colours are applied in transparent washes that give a fresh delicate luminosity to any subject. Almost perfect examples of the medium are seen in the work of Russell Flint, admittedly the works of this master are not antique, but they are well worth examination in the interest of knowledge.

Water colours were used many centuries before the discovery of oil paint, the pigment applied either in washes, or as tempera. Tempera, which is powder colour mixed with a binder, was a generally used technique until about the 15th century for easel pictures. The binder was either egg white, or the yolk or even a combined mixture of both.

Techniques employed in water-colours, in addition to tempera, include colour washes used in conjunction with pencil line drawings, which produces a fine, delicate, compact picture, or a loose, free style, dependent upon the mood of the artist. Opaque water-colours mixed with solid opaque white were used on a tinted paper, giving a strong, vigorous picture. This technique was a little like oil painting, because the colours could be applied thickly, and pale colours could be applied over darker colours or vice versa.

Painting in oil, "The Discussion" by O. Benedilct. A minor master that can be collected relatively inexpensively.
(*D. C. Gohm*)

Some of the finest water-colours have been produced using a combination of both transparent washes and opaque colour.

The most prominent name in " early " English water-colours is Paul Sandby (1725–1809), who was a topographical draughtsman, employed by the Crown. It is not surprising, therefore, that his landscapes are meticulous. Opaque colour, or gouache, was a medium used extensively, and very expertly, by Sandby.

This artist was the first to produce aquatints in this country (See Prints) and was also responsible for a series of etching including Hyde Park, and Windsor views.

Samuel Prout (1783–1852) was born in Plymouth, and much of his work was executed on the continent. His style is bold, but very controlled, lending itself admirably to the art of lithography (See Prints), a process used by Prout extensively for illustrative works including " Sketches in France, Switzerland, and Italy " and " Facsimiles of Sketches made in Flanders and Germany ".

Prout's water-colours have been copied extensively, therefore his so called signature on the picture is no guarantee that it is an original.

Thomas Rowlandson (1756–1827) was a water-colourist with an interest mainly centred on man and his pursuits, rather than his environment. He is often considered to be the first cartoonist of his day. His water-colour sketches, although invariably drawn with a subtle delicacy, have the exaggerated and inelegant quality associated with caricature.

Rowlandson prepared a large number of designs for books, and was also a celebrated etcher. His technique was to first produce the original watercolour, and then etch the main features in outline on a copper plate, which was subsequently finished, and aquatinted, or coloured, by others in imitation of the original.

A typical work by Rowlandson named " Brook Green Fair " can be seen at the Victoria and Albert museum.

William Henry Hunt (1790–1864) was a well known painter of flowers, fruit and vegetables, which he painted in exquisite detail.

Clarkson Stanfield (1793–1867) was a very competent artist mainly concerning himself with sea and landscapes.

David Cox (1783–1859). Much of Cox's work was executed in North Wales, but he also visited Holland, France, and Belgium. His style was vigorous, broad and full of charm. He liked to work on a kind of wrapping paper which had a slightly rough, tinted texture, ideally suited to his style. A similar type of paper can be obtained to day, and is known as " Cox Paper ".

There are many other very competent water-colour artists worthy of study, and their names are as follows:—

Francis Towne	(1740–1816)
William Pars	(1742–1782)
Thomas Hearne	(1744–1817)
Edward Dayes	(1763–1804)
Thomas Girton	(1775–1802)
John Robert Cozens	(1752–1797)
John Sell Cotman	(1782–1842)
Peter De Wint	(1784–1849)

You may not be able to afford many paintings by the above artists, but nevertheless, they should be studied so that a standard of quality can be established, which will greatly assist in the evaluation of works by less exalted artists.

GLASS PICTURES

Early glass pictures were produced by a process known as verre eglomisé, which is glass decorated on the underside with gold and silver foils; and by gold glass etching. Both of these processes are very old, and may even go back to Roman times. These pictures are unlikely to interest a new collector, so we will commence with the 17th and 18th century silhouettes.

Silhouettes were either painted on the back of the glass and backed with a coloured pigment, or they were painted on the reverse side of convex or flat glass and mounted with a white card at the back. The silhouettes on convex glass are most interesting, because the actual painting is raised from the background and so casts a shadow. If buying such pictures inspect them carefully, for they may not be actually backpainted, but made from silhouettes cut out and pasted onto the glass.

There are also many silhouettes painted on card and mounted under glass. Whilst these may be of interest to a collector of silhouettes, they cannot really be considered a glass picture, but if the silhouette has an elgomisé border then it can qualify.

The 17th century method of making glass pictures involved the use of a print, most of these seem to have religious subjects and are not in very great demand, but there were some very attractive decorative prints used if you can find them. I once had a beautiful example of " Nelson ", and I have seen a very attractive set of " The Seasons ". The process involved soaking the print as yet uncoloured in water to remove the body, or size. When the print had been dried it was stuck, face-down, onto a sheet of glass and left to dry. Now came the operation requiring considerable skill—the paper was moistened and carefully rubbed away to leave only the thinnest film of paper carrying the printed impression.

When thoroughly dry the back of the print was then coloured. If you look at the back of such a picture, you will note that the tone value of the colours vary from those viewed from the front, due to the effect of print and glass.

The earlier the picture of this type, the better the painting, later ones tend to be more crudely executed.

MINIATURES

Miniature portrait paintings have always been in demand, both by collectors and folk with an eye for interior decoration. When used for decoration, they are shown to their best advantage if hung in a compact group, or one above the other, on a suitable wall. They can also be displayed in a glass-fronted cabinet.

Miniatures, or " limnings ", as they are named, really became established as an art form about 1540 when Holbein turned his attention to painting small circular portraits on vellum with opaque watercolours. The 16th century miniatures were also painted on playing cards, which made an excellent support.

During the 17th century, the portrait miniature underwent an evolutionary change from an alliance with medieval illuminators to an alliance with contemporary oil painting. A few miniatures of this period will be found painted in oil and possibly on metal.

It was during the early part of the 18th century that ivory was introduced as a ground and support, the natural colour of ivory was an ideal background when used with transparent water-colour.

Nicholas Hilliar (1547–1619) is one of the best known of our English miniaturists. His fame stems from his wonderful portraits of Queen Elizabeth, and from 1584 he was granted " the sole rights " to paint her portraits in miniature. Much of this artist's work has been reproduced countless times.

Other 17th century miniaturists are John Hoskins, Samuel Cooper, Isaac Oliver, Thomas Flatman and Nicholas Dixon.

About the turn of the 18th century we will find miniatures painted by Lawrence Cross, Bernard Lens, and later in the century by Gervase Spence, Samuel Cotes, Nathaniel Hone and Luke Sullivan. Between the late 18th and early 19th century the dominant artists were Richard Cosway, George Engleheart and John Smart.

Any miniatures by the above artists will be difficult to find and will certainly be expensive.

Miniature paintings are not restricted to English origin. The American continent followed the English example, and their earliest listed painter was John Watson of East Jersey. Little appears to be known about the subject prior to this artist.

The American artists of note are Charles Willson Peale, Joseph Dunkerley, Nathaniel Hancock, Henry Benbridge and many others.

An interesting series of portraits was painted by Charles Willson Peale during the war of Independence, these were mainly officers and included George Washington.

It is worth seeking American miniatures, but they are rare in England, American collectors often have to be satisfied with miniatures of European origin.

Apart from the " big named " artists, there are many other very competent artists who have produced excellent examples of the art which can be bought for a relatively few pounds. Use your judgement—if the quality is good, and the picture pleases you—buy it! If, however, you wish to study the work of miniaturists of the late 19th and early 20th century, then here are a few suggested artists worthy of attention.

John Cox Dillman Engleheart (1784–1862)
A popular artist of his period, often painted backgrounds of trees, flowers etc., on his miniature portraits.

Sir William John Newton (1785–1869)
There was a tendency by this artist to use a brown shading on the face of his portraits. His work is usually signed on the back.

Sir William Charles Ross, R.A. (1794–1860)
An outstanding 19th century miniaturist, who is reputed to have painted over 2,200 portraits. He was appointed Miniature Painter to the Queen in 1837, and painted many portraits of the Royal Family.

Simon Jacques Rochard (1788–1872)
A French artist who came to England in 1815.

Reginald Easton (1807–93)
Although a self taught artist, he became a notable artist in water-colour and in miniatures. Noted for his child portraits.

John Haslem (1808–84)

There are not many miniatures to be found by this artist, probably it was not his main vocation. He is better known for his association with porcelain.

William Egley (1798–1870)

His miniatures are said to have a slight resemblance to those by Sir William Charles Ross, but they lack the fine quality of his composition.

John Linnell (1792–1882)

John Linnell is better known for his landscape paintings, a subject he preferred to portraiture, therefore, miniatures by him are relatively scarce.

Having acquired a few miniatures, give them the care they deserve. Do not let them dry out by hanging them too near a fire. If you do the ivory is likely to buckle and distort. Neither hang them where they receive the full rays of the sun, this will cause them to fade just like any other water-colour.

SILK PICTURES

Just over 100 years ago, the weaving industry in Coventry found itself in the grip of a slump, mainly caused by the importation of foreign goods. Thomas Stevens, who had until this time been a ribbon weaver of world renown, found himself with the possibility of closing down his works. It has been quoted that necessity is the mother of invention, and in this instance it certainly proved to be an apt quotation. Instead of bemoaning his fate, Stevens set about modifying his Jacquard looms for the production of bookmarkers, silk pictures and novelties.

This new venture proved to be an instant success, and soon Stevens had an overwhelming order book. By virtue of the small size, approximately postcard size or less, the picture could be despatched readily to anywhere in the world by post.

Although the novelties and bookmarks of Thomas Stevens are well worth collecting, it is his pictures that are in great demand. These pictures are known as " Stevenographs ", and they are beautifully woven and brilliantly coloured pictures on silk, mounted on card with a bevelled, rectangular opening to frame them. On the back of the card, Stevens stuck a label which stated that he was the " Sole Inventor and Manufacturer ". Listed on this label was a range of available subjects, and that the price was a shilling unframed, and two shillings and sixpence if required in a Gold Oxford frame. This latter price included packing in a box! You will be very lucky to-day if you find anyone even willing to part with a " Stevenograph ", if you do they will not be cheap, and may not be in an acceptable condition.

It is almost impossible to date a Stevenograph with any degree of accuracy. The pictures were produced in the form of a long ribbon, or bolt, and mounted as required by demand. Consequently the stock of bolts could be stored for many years, causing possible deterioration in the brilliance of colour.

Approximately one hundred and fifty different subjects have been produced, covering an extremely wide variety, but irrespective of the subject, they are all very worthwhile collectors items.

The safest way of ensuring that you have a Stevenograph is to make certain the trade label is pasted to the back, the name woven into the silk, or printed on the front of the mount.

Thomas Stevens never covered his process with copyright, and like most successful ventures, he had his imitators.

He created his early bookmarks about 1860–1880, a period when ribbons were first mounted for framing. At this time similar ribbon pictures were appearing from the looms of competitors, such as Odell and French; Ratcliff and Son; and Willie Grant, but the work of these weavers were mainly in black and white, although they did produce occasional colour pictures.

As a general guide to age, the list of advertised subjects on the trade label will give an indication—the fewer subjects listed, the earlier the example.

Like prints, the subject will greatly influence availability and price: early trains, coaching and American subjects are, no doubt, the most expensive.

Back of Stevenograph. Woven Silk Picture showing typical trade label and subjects listed for sale.
(*Photo by D. Gohm*)

PAPIER MÂCHÉ

Papier mâché was invented by the French, and as the name suggests it is literally mashed or pulped paper. The original papier mâché centre was Paris, probably because it was a city where the raw material could be had in abundance, due to the excessive advertising carried out by bill posters which were continually being renewed and changed.

Papier mâché is not the delicate material that the name would imply, and many lasting articles were made from it, however it does lack the durability of wood and metals, consequently much of it has been destroyed by ill use and bad handling in storage.

There were two basic methods of producing articles from papier mâché. The method known as the French style involved the use of high grade paper pulp, or good quality fibrous paper, the oatmeal-like pulp was then poured into a mould which hardened under the influence of a slow heat. The English method of making papier mâché was usually formed by pasting individual layers of paper together, forming a very strong laminate. The laminate was very suitable for the manufacture of such articles as tables, trays, chairs and other articles requiring some inherent strength.

The manufacture of articles in paper pulp commenced about 1765 in Britain, and at about this time small articles were being produced in the French manner.

Henry Clay of Birmingham, a japanner, probably laid the corner stone for the industry in England in 1772 when he took out a patent for laminated sheets of paper formed by pasting individual sheets together. Being a japanner, Clay's interest in the material was sparked by its suitability for japanning. Japanning, a technique of Eastern origin, is a method of painting wood or metals by grounds of opaque colours in varnish; these ground colours were subsequently covered with several coats of clear japan varnish, requiring stoving to obtain the beautiful surface lustre characteristic of the technique. The problem was to prevent wood, which was one of the common basic materials of the period, from warping or even splitting during the stoving process. The English style of papier mâché overcame this problem, and also presented a hard, smooth surface ideally suited to the application of the pigments.

Clay sold his products under the name of Paper Ware. He used a special sheet of paper which was greenish in colour and resembled blotting paper but was probably a little thicker, the name for this paper was Making paper.

It is surprising to find the number of uses that Henry Clay found for his new material, apart from the obvious small boxes, tea trays and waiters, he included panels or roofs for coaches, sedan chairs, panels for rooms, and even

Papier mâché snuff box, metal lined.
(*Aldate Ltd.*)

doors and cabins of ships. By the early part of the 19th century, manufacturing techniques and the materials had improved which made it possible to mould the material without the disadvantages of bubbling, found in the early French techniques of moulding.

C. F. Bielefeld, of London, took out a patent in 1845 that widened the application of papier mâché by using it for internal decoration in conjunction with the architect. The Victorians used the material to produce their period ceilings, in skilful imitation of the conventional plaster of paris mouldings. Specialist manufacturers supplied cornice mouldings, central roses and a great variety of general border designs.

From a collector's point of view papier mâché is a Victorian product, although it was used in China many centuries ago. It offers the collector of modest means an interesting subject, that can satisfy the collecting instinct and at the same time decorate the home. Good pieces will be difficult to find, much of these have found their way to the United States, but it can however still be found but may require a diligent search.

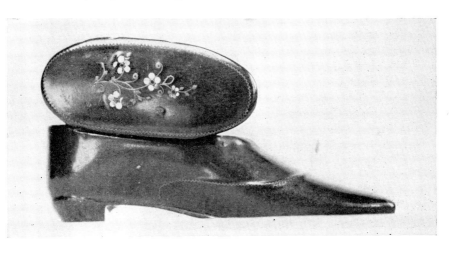

Papier mâché snuff box in the form of a shoe. Lid inlaid with design in Mother-of-Pearl.
(*Loco Antiques*)

PEWTER

Pewter is a tin based alloy, with minor additions of lead, antimony, copper and bismuth which are added in small proportions. There have been many varieties of pewter used in the past and it is almost impossible to be certain of the type used for any specific piece.

In general terms, Fine Old pewter had one hundred and twelve parts tin to twenty-six parts copper. Plate pewter had one hundred parts tin, eight parts antimony, four parts copper, and four parts bismuth. Superior pewter had one hundred parts tin and seventeen parts antimony. Ley metal had eighty parts tin and twenty parts lead. It will be seen therefore, that the main constituent of pewter is tin, and that very little lead was ever used.

English pewter dates back to the 10th century and was used until the 19th century, but it was not until after the Restoration that it came into general use. It was not before the middle of the 18th century that the wealth of England permitted the houses of the day to replace their wooden utensils with pewter, but from then on, over the best part of a hundred years, pewter became the material for everyday commodities and utensils.

It was used in churches for alms dishes, alms plates and sacramental vessels. It was used in the dwelling houses to provide basins, bowls, ink-stands, candlesticks, mantle ornaments, snuff boxes, tankards, spoons, plates and flagons. English pewter derives its appeal mainly from its good proportions, and functional design. Decoration played only a minor role in the overall presentation.

Touch Marks

A touch mark in pewter does not carry the same authority as the hall marks used on gold and silver. A true hall mark used on precious metals refers to material quality and date of manufacture, they do not encompass the design or workmanship. Pewter touchmarks have no special value apart from interest and as a guide to their maker, they do not refer in any way to the quality of the alloy. In many instances dates will appear in the touches but this will not date the article, it represents the year of registration with the London Guild and not the year of manufacture, but if we know the approximate date of the death of the manufacturer we can at least obtain the period, i.e. it will be somewhere between the date of registration and the demise of the maker.

Pewterers would sometimes add additional touches resembling hall marks. These were usually four in number which closely resembled those used on silver plate. These bogus hall marks were not supported in law, or by the Pewterers Guild.

Here are a few examples of touch marks.

Thomas King.	Two hands supporting an anchor displayed in a large oval with a crown above. (1675)
Thomas Deacon.	Flaming beacon in a large oval with a moulded rim and palm leaves. (1780).
Adam Tate.	Outline of a cross with castle in the middle and the initials A.T. on either side. (1747)
Henry Adams.	Figures of Adam and Eve.
John Cambridge.	Heart surmounting a book with palm leaves. (1687)
Robert Nicholson.	Eagle on a globe surrounded by palm leaves. (1690)
John Barlow.	Tulip above a plough. (1698)
Thomas Mathews.	Mermaid and six roundels with palm leaves. (1711).
Robert Patience.	Standing figure of Queen with sceptre. (1771)
John Wingod.	Square and compass. (1748)
Paul Fisher.	Fisherman in a boat. (1798)

Cleaning

There are many diverse opinions regarding the best method to clean pewter, or even whether it should be cleaned at all. This is a matter for personal taste, if the article is in good condition it will usually be sufficient to wipe it with a soft cloth dipped in paraffin oil, lightly dusted with powdered whiting. The finished sheen can be applied by polishing with a chamois leather.

Stains and blotches caused by oxidization can usually be removed by a long soak in domestic paraffin. Badly scaled and pock marked surfaces may need the action of an acid, and as most acids are difficult and often dangerous to use, it is better to gain a little experience on the easier methods, using modern detergents and chemicals before resorting to the rather drastic treatment by acids. Badly scaled pewter can first be treated with a fine wire wool, this may cause minor scratches that have to be removed, using a finer abrasive such as rouge or plate powder, or by using the proprietary item Dura-Glit. Always use plenty of this wool and then polish with a dry cloth before the surface is completely dry.

When starting your collection, the temptation to buy any odd piece of pewter that comes your way will be irresistible, but very soon you will feel the need to specialise.

Here are a few suggestions.

You can choose dishes, chargers, plates or flagons: tankards, beakers or bowls. These articles are known as hollow-ware, or if you wish to have a wider choice, collect articles that would normally stand on a table, such as candlesticks, salt-cellars, ink-wells, coasters and so on, or on a broader basis specialise in household, ecclesiastical or tavern pieces.

There is of course some very fine pewter other than that of English origin. There is Scottish, Flemish, German, French and American, therefore, you could select the country of origin as a theme for your collection.

GLOSSARY

Akerne: This means Acorn-like. Early 15th century spoons were decorated with an acorn-like knob and described in mediaeval times as 'With an Akerne'.

Alloy: A mixture of metals, usually a base metal, to which has been added a metal of finer quality.

Ampulla: A flask, goblet, or small phial mainly used to hold water or oils for sacred purposes.

Ball & Claw: Describes the shape of a foot displaying a ball held in an eagle's or lion's talon.

Baluster: This refers to the shape seen in a balustrade, it usually means the graceful swelling central curve, seen in the form of a stem of a candlestick, a stemmed cup or the body of a flagon or measure. (Characterised by having a bellied middle).

Beaker: This is from the old English word " Biker ", usually a tapered sided, or lipped drinking vessel; describes drinking pots and cups.

Black Metal: Pewter with a greater proportion of lead to tin than is normally found in domestic pewter, generally used for organ pipes.

Booge: The part of a plate or dish between the rim and the base which provides the dished configuration.

Bossed: Dishes with raised centre portions are said to be bossed.

Capstan: In the 17th century and early 18th centuries salt-cellars and pewter ink-wells of a late style were made in a conical form with a broad base, resembling that of a ship's capstan. These salt-cellars were known as ' Capstan Salts '.

Cardinal's Hat: One of the earliest forms of a pewter dish usually around 15″–16″ in diameter resembling an inverted Cardinal's hat.

Cassolette: A perfume burner consisting of a bowl with a pierced lid.

Chargers: Dishes usually larger than 13″ in diameter.

Chased: Decoration carried out with a lining tool or punch.

Chopin: Derived from the French word " chopine " meaning a pint. It was used to denote the capacity of Scottish spirit measures.

Coaster: Tray for a decanter or drinking vessel, used to prevent the rough bottom of the bottle scratching the wooden table tops.

Cupping Dish: Dishes used by the surgeons for bloodletting; concentric rings inside the bowl were there to measure the amount of blood released.

Ecuelle: Generally a kitchen or scullery utensil such as a porringer or bowl.

Hammerhead: A low, heavy, thumb piece used for balluster measure of the 1690's, not unlike the head of a carpenter's claw hammer.

Haystack or Harvester: A wine and spirit measure made by Irish Pewterers from about 1820. They resemble a circular haystack in shape.

Hollow-ware: As the name suggests, articles of capacity such as pots, tankards and bowls.

Mutchkin: Meaning a little cap. A type of tappit hen, i.e. Scottish measure smaller than a chopin.

Patina: Patina is the term used to describe the finish of pewter surfaces, either obtained by continual handling, age, or by ceaseless rubbing with a soft cloth.

Planish: To flatten and smooth by hammering, the action of hammering also hardened the pewter surface.

Pounce Box: A pewter container, not unlike a modern pepper-pot. This container was used to hold pumice which was sprinkled on to newly written correspondence to dry the ink.

Pricket: A candlestick terminating in a spike, which fitted into the base of the candle itself.

Quaich: A shallow saucer or bowl with two handles. This vessel was mainly of Scottish origin.

Repousse: Decoration obtained by hammering from the underside of pewter articles, i.e. raised by beating up.

Spout Pot: Any pot with a projecting spout.

Tappit-Hen: A type of Scottish measure. Name is derived from the old French word "Topynett" meaning a quart. Most tappit-hens have bun or domed lids but the Aberdeen type in common with the Irish Harvester is lidless.

Touch Plates: Touches, Touch Blocks. These were in fact early trade marks, the plates of pewter upon which members of the Guild had to strike their personal touches on admission into their Guild. The touch plates were kept at the Guild Headquarters, and used for tracing makers in the event of their wares being below the Guild Standards.

PINCHBECK

A typical dictionary definition of the word " Pinch-beck " is a zinc and copper alloy; cheap jewellery; counterfeit, sham, flashy or tawdry. Articles so described seem out of place in a book on antiques, but you should know something about them, who knows, you may find them of sufficient interest to collect. Many people do so.

The word " Pinchbeck " is derived from the name of two brothers, Christopher and Edward Pinchbeck, who, for nearly a hundred years, between 1670 and approximately 1766, produced useful articles in a comparatively cheap alloy for the masses, in imitation of the more expensive pieces using gold and silver. This new alloy, discovered by Christopher, closely approximated gold and could be worked much the same way as gold and at a glance could be mistaken for the real thing. With this material they produced rings, bracelets, necklaces and jewellery sets, using the cheaper gems. Watch-chains, snuff-boxes, shoe-buckles, patch-boxes, watch-cases, sword belts, whip handles, cane heads, small frames, coat buttons, salvers, and so on.

It was stated by the Pinchbeck brothers that this new alloy of theirs was in fact untarnishable, it may well have been during their day, and there are some very nice un-tarnished pieces to this day to prove it; unfortunately two hundred years of exposure to normal atmospheric pollution has caused much of it to become darkened.

The majority of Pinchbeck is attractive, and it is often enhanced with pieces of onyx, agate, lapis-lazuli, and red agate.

Because the base material of Pinchbeck is cheap, one should not conclude that the finished articles lacked quality, they were produced most skilfully, with great attention to detail.

Pinchbeck will not cost you a lot of money, neither will a collection, at least at this time, appreciate very much in value. However, who is to say what will happen in the future? Fashions change, and in a few years we might find Pinchbeck highly regarded, and the pieces we can now buy for shillings may cost us pounds. Some experience is required when buying, make certain that you buy old pinchbeck, there have been many modern imitators. The modern pinchbeck is not so good as the old, as you will soon find out when you have gained the necessary experience.

POTTERY AND PORCELAIN

Bow

The Bow factory, situated on the eastern outskirts of London, started production sometime in 1744, or very near that date. It was certainly producing by 1750.

In 1744, Thomas Frye, a painter and engraver, together with his partner E. Heylyn, took out a patent for the manufacture of porcelain using imported clay from America. In 1748 Frye took out a second patent which added bone-ash to the formula. This addition is now useful because the resultant phosphoric acid can now be detected by chemical analysis, and the presence of bone ash proved. While this is not conclusive evidence that a particular example came from the Bow factory, it does narrow the field of possibilities to those factories using this material.

Thomas Frye managed the factory until 1759, from 1763 the progress of the factory is a little obscure, but it is known that it was finally acquired by William Duesbury, of Derby, who continued to operate the factory until about 1776, when it was closed finally and the moulds removed to Derby.

The Bow factory specialised in useful wares, such as plates and dishes, but not exclusively so, many figures were made also. Not very much is known about the early wares, but an inkwell in the Victoria and Albert Museum decorated with sprays of flowers in the Chinese style, is inscribed " Made at New Canton 1751 " which indicates an effort to compete with Eastern importation at that time.

The majority of surviving useful wares are decorated with underglaze blue.

Transfer painting in russet and a purplish black was employed about 1756 and early colour, up to about 1765, included famille rose and Kakiemen style painting, which was practised extensively.

Bow figures have small doll-like heads, receding chins and slight modelling of the cheeks, and upturned noses, often having floral bocages at the back and mounted on a base ornamented by scrolls. After about 1760, enamelled examples became more florid, and were marked sometimes with an anchor and dagger, painted in red. Later porcelain became rather chalky, with a less compact texture, consequently it was lighter in weight than the earlier examples.

Bow is a soft paste porcelain, cream in colour, with a tendency to stain brown where the glaze has been chipped, or worn away, and occasionally has black specking.

Delftware

Delftware is a name so Dutch in flavour that it is surprising to find that Delftware was not originally a product of the Netherlands. It originated in Moorish Spain and Renaissance Italy, travelling on its way through Majorca, where it collected the general description of Maiolica. (The name first used in Italy for the lustred wares of Valencia, now a 19th century English name used to describe lead glazed pottery).

Delftware was produced both in England and Flanders a considerable time prior to the establishment of the Delft potteries. Guido Andries, a maiolica potter, worked in Antwerp about 1508 and this date is generally accepted as the beginning of maiolica pottery in the Southern Netherlands. About 1550 the Antwerp potters moved further North and in 1567 Jasper Andries, either a son or grandson of Guido Andries, moved to England. This dispersion of maiolica potters has resulted in the two schools of pottery known as " Dutch Delft " and " English Delftware ". The rise of Delft as a pottery centre dates approximately from 1650, and from this period until the middle of the 18th century, Delft attained its greatest growth, and was in its most prosperous period.

The material of Delftware is not stoneware, porcelain, or china, it is a soft earthenware with a lead glaze that has been made opaque with the addition of oxide of tin, or ashes. Painting the designs on this white, absorbent glaze required deftness and a very confident hand. Once the colour had been applied it sank into the surface with a degree of permanence that made corrections difficult, if not impossible.

The Netherlands improved the basic techniques by covering the painted design with an additional lead glaze which added richness, the whole piece was then fired at a high temperature, to " set " both glazes simultaneously. Further decoration may then have been added in more delicate colours, and then the piece again fired, but now at a lower temperature. This is, in fact, an enamelling process, and compares with similar techniques used on china, porcelain and opaque glass. Early Netherlands dishes and plates were often tin enamelled on the front face only, the under surface being glazed with a transparent lead glaze, through which could be seen the grey-yellow clay.

The influx of Chinese porcelain, brought by merchant ships around the Cape into Italy, inspired the Italian potters, with their Oriental designs of the Ming dynasty, and the influences of the Near and Middle East. Although obviously affected by these influences they nevertheless developed their own styles whilst making similar wares.

The marks on Delftware are numerous, though the early marks, which were fewer, have proved to be unreliable. From about 1680 onwards, when the industry began to form larger groups, marking became more predominant and it is believed that these marks are indicative of pottery owners, or lessees of potteries.

Delft pottery was mainly produced in the familiar blue and white throughout the 18th century, the Oriental influence being modified by the drapery of Baroque motifs, followed by the profused ornamentation of Rococo. Earlier wares copied the cobalt blue decoration used by the Ming potters, because of its suitability for high temperature firing, an important factor in porcelain manufacture.

Delftware was not only produced in blue and white, from the late 17th century it was also produced using a copper-green, iron-red, and a yellow, the latter colour being somewhat rare, and the red being a new colour in

European ceramics. These colours required high temperature firing and were fired in the kiln simultaneously with the tin glaze. From about 1720, the process of enamelling by firing additional colours over the glaze at a low temperature, increased the range of colours by adding greys, opaque, blues, pinks and lilac.

English Delftware, as previously stated, started in 1567 with Jasper Andries. He is reputed to have settled in Norwich with a fellow compatriot, named Jacob Janson, but not being able to find suitable materials in the vicinity for making his apothecaries mortars and equipment, tiles and so on, petitioned Elizabeth I for a permit to move his operation to London. This was granted, and in the year 1571 the partners were settled in Aldgate. It was not long before Flemish, Dutch and English potters joined the community, to start the centre of English Delftware making.

The earliest tin-glazed earthenware produced at Lambeth is estimated to be about 1665, when John Ariens van Hamme, a Delft potter, established his works there.

Bristol, famous for its glass, was also the home of many kinds of pottery, not excluding Delft, which it is estimated was first produced in the village of Brislington in 1650 by John Bissick and Robert Fleming.

Delftware was made at Liverpool from about 1716 by Alderman Thomas Shaw. Other early Liverpool potters were Zacharial Barnes, Richard Chaffers, the Pennington brothers, and Philip Christian.

A well known product of Liverpool were their charpots.

Dutch potters were at one time much concerned with making articles that could be used, rather than purely just as ornamental pieces, such as salt cellars, pepper castors, butter dishes, plates, soup tureens and general tableware.

Ornamental figures and animal pieces of horses, frogs, cocks, hens, parrots and cats have been modelled in Delftware, but generally they lack in quality, probably due to the deficiency of modelling skill of most of the potters.

Tiles constitute one of the main items suitable for collectors. These were used in the Netherlands for walls of kitchens, dairies, fireplaces, wainscotings, and cellars, designed as individual tiles, or with patterns that could be used in continuation. Early tiles were decorated with pomegranates, and clusters of grapes, flowers and animals, followed later with vases of flowers.

Tiles were coloured with the typical blue, also green, yellow and orange. Occasionally manganese purple was added. The body colour of early tiles was reddish, later they became buff and were made much thinner.

Tiles produced during the latter part of the 17th century make ideal collectors items with their attractively designed sea monsters, ships, views and figures of fishermen, farmers, tumblers and groups of figures.

Flower vases, candlesticks, goblets, money boxes, wall pockets, teapots, drug and apothecaries jars, plates, food-warmers, mugs, puzzle jars, bowls and jugs, and wine-bin labels, have all been made in Delftware.

Doulton

Doulton ware was made from about 1820 to 1854 under the trade name of " Doulton & Watts ", then John Watts retired, and Henry Doulton continued under the name of " Doulton & Co. " The products under the Watts partnership were mainly industrial and utilitarian, but some stoneware jugs and ornamental bottles were also manufactured.

In 1862, Henry Doulton turned his attention to decorated pottery, but his early attempts were not very successful; however, he employed students from the Lambeth School of Art to decorate his pottery, and exhibited at the South Kensington Exhibition of 1871. From this time onwards, Doultons new Art Pottery was established.

The Doulton stoneware, made at Lambeth, was a fine quality, salt-glazed stoneware, and most examples carry the personal mark of the decorator, factory mark, and in many instances, the date of manufacture.

Henry Doulton was one of the first potters to employ

Four pieces of salt glazed stoneware, one on right by Florence E. Barlow, others by Hannah B. Barlow. Biscuit Barrel 1879   Covered Jar C. 1892–1899   Jug 1879   Vase 1883 (*Doulton & Co. Ltd.*)

SALT-GLAZED STONEWARE
Vase 15½″ high, incised Cows, Horses, Child. White slip; 1881. Hannah B. Barlo w
(*Doulton & Co. Ltd.*)
Vase 17½″ high, incised Cattle, Horses. White slip; 1883. Hannah B.
Barlow and L. A. Barlow (in Mr. Gee's possession).
(*Doulton & Co. Ltd.*)

Stoneware Vase; salt-glaze (brown) M.V. Marshall, 1875. 9″ high.
(Doulton & Co. Ltd.)

female labour on a large scale, he recruited the majority of these artists from students who were studying in the Government design schools. They were permitted to express themselves by practising their own individual styles. This was a very successful venture, some of the students eventually gained a national reputation.

In addition to salt glazed stoneware, the Lambeth factory produced tiles and architectural terra-cotta work; these were used for decorative features on buildings and for mantelpieces and hearths. Another interesting feature was used in making " Chine " ware, the body was patterned whilst still soft by impressing it with a fabric material, which gave the example of a woven pattern. Other bodies used were named " Impasto ", " Silicon ",

Salt-glaze frog group by George Tinworth entitled "Going to the Derby", 3¼" high. 1886.
(*Doulton & Co. Ltd.*)

Three salt-glaze Doulton Ware jugs designed (l. to r.) George Tinworth
C. 1874, Arthur B. Barlow 1873, and George Tinworth C. 1874. The
colourings are browns, cobalt blues and cream.
(*Doulton & Co. Ltd.*)

" Carrara ", and " Marqueterie " and " Doulton
Faience ".

Faience was introduced about 1873 and was decorated
by painting, unlike the stoneware, which was mainly
incised, or modelled. The production of stoneware at
Lambeth was discontinued in March 1956.

Collecting Lambeth made Doulton provides a relatively inexpensive field for a new collector and the number
of examples available is still sufficiently large to allow
some discrimination.

An excellent collection can be formed from examples

Miscellaneous group of carved ivory figures.

A Small selection of genuine Goss crested china.

Martinware grotesque Bird Group, with removeable heads.
(*Southall Central Library*)

Martinware miniature vases, note size compared with halfpenny.
(*Southall Central Library*)

decorated by one of the many known artists, or by collecting only early pieces.

George Tinworth for example, modelled beautiful
figures, etc. Other artists worthy of mention are Hannah
B. Barlow, Frank A. Butler, Edith D. Lupton, Frances E.
Lee, Louisa E. Edwards, Florence E. Barlow and many
others.

Goss China

Goss china is not strictly an antique. Since by general
definition an antique is required to be over 100 years old,
Goss china is only half this age, but it is fast becoming
established as a collectors item, and no excuse is offered
for its inclusion here as a " young antique ".

This fine quality white porcelain ware was made by
William Henry Goss, from Stoke-on-Trent, Staffordshire,
and decorated with beautiful coloured coats of arms of
every English town of importance. Pieces were also
produced featuring a few Scottish and Irish towns.
These were sold cheaply as souvenirs around the turn of
the last century, and were brought back from holidays,
or a day at the coast, as presents for friends and family.
They ornamented articles such as tiny jugs, spill holders,
small vases, ash trays, stud boxes, models of houses, small
flat plates, mugs, and a host of other smallish items.

Falcon Potteries were started by W. H. Goss in 1858
to manufacture parian holloware, which is a fine grained,
waxy feldspathic resembling white marble, mainly for
use in the boudoir. These pieces were delicately
decorated with floral patterns.

In 1890, Goss developed a variety of porcelain which
was ivory in colour, had a waxy sheen and was ideally
suited as a base for presenting the coat of arms which
were enamelled over the glaze. The credit for the
enamelling process goes to Goss's son Adolphus. W. H.
Goss made crested china in his early days as a potter,
but these were not accepted by the buying public. Probably the crests, originally restricted to public schools and
universities, could only be identified personally by a
minority.

Genuine Goss porcelain has a quality of its own. Many imitations may be seen in junk shops, market stalls, and even antique shops, but will be found to be of inferior quality. All Goss china bears his mark—a rising falcon —look for this before parting with your money.

As a guide to age, from 1891 the trade mark of the falcon had the word " England " superimposed under it and either " W. H. Goss " or " W.H.G."

The more valuable pieces of Goss are the larger items, or those depicting two or more coats of arms.

Now is the time to start with Goss, it is very cheap, but it will not be long before this relatively new field has claimed the attention of a considerable number of new collectors, and the present " easy market " will dry up.

Martin Ware

Martin Ware was produced over a relatively limited

The four Martin Brothers at work in their pottery.
(*Southall Central Library*)

period, from 1873 to about 1914, by the four Martin Brothers, and although their wares may not rank with some of the more universally known potters for quality, their style and character were so individual that they have now become very collectable items.

The four brothers worked as a team, dividing their labours to suit their individual skills. Their workshop was a studio, and they are considered to be among the earliest of the studio potters.

The team leader was Robert Wallace Martin (1843–1923). Some of his better known works included a series of ornaments in bird forms, these were grotesque caricatures of birds, invariably with large beaks, some of which had removable heads. He also produced other animal forms.

Walter Martin (1859–1912) concentrated on making the large vases, and the production processes of firing and mixing the clay. Edwin Martin (1860–1915) was the artist-decorator working in relief and incised designs, with floral, fish, and seaweed motifs.

Charles Martin (d. 1910) was in charge of their retail shop in Brownlow Street, Holborn, but he also assumed the role of general administrator.

The Martin Brothers worked initially in Fulham, then London, and finally in Southall, and their wares are marked by incising the soft clay before firing, with their name, place of manufacture and numeries to denote month and year made.

Martin Ware is a salt-glazed stoneware, and the majority is a darkish brown colour. Varied and interesting examples of this unique ware can be seen at Southall Central Library.

Minton

Minton is a world famous name that immediately suggests fine, elegant, porcelain. It is highly regarded, and the name alone is sufficient to " hall-mark " it for quality.

Thomas Minton (1765–1836) was an apprentice of Thomas Turner at the Caughley porcelain works, where he trained as an engraver. In 1793 he founded the firm, at Stoke-on-Trent, that was later to become known all over the world. The pottery, however, did not start producing until 1796, its early examples were of earthenware, usually unmarked, and decorated with blue printed designs in underglazes.

Porcelain production followed after about two years, but the majority of these wares were unmarked. It was not until about 1805 that the first articles were marked.

It is interesting to note that porcelain was not made between about 1817 and 1823.

The early porcelains produced from about 1805 to 1816 were marked with a painted letter " L ", sometimes with a number underneath, to indicate the pattern number.

Tea and dessert services, and other fine pieces made at this time, were beautifully decorated with floral patterns by artists Joseph Bancroft, George Hancock, and Thomas Steel.

Identification of Minton porcelain produced during the 1820's and 1830's is extremely difficult for the layman as it was normally unmarked. Factory pattern and design books show the examples produced during this period but they are not normally easily accessible, although a few sample pages have been reproduced in text books.

Between 1820 and about 1850, both ornamental and useful wares were produced in literally hundreds of different forms, and decorated in numerous styles. A decorative feature very popular then, and avidly collected now, were floral encrusted pieces. This was a form of embellishment using applied modelled flowers in great profusion, exquisitely coloured. Jugs, vases and ornamental bottles were popular subjects.

Minton also produced fine quality figures, busts, and groups. These were made in glazed and enamel porcelain, and in the bisque—unglazed or " biscuit " porcelain.

Collecting antique Minton is expensive, and requires a little expert knowledge, but do not be put off, it is still possible to find later examples at a reasonable price, but you may have to search very hard.

Parian

Parian ware first appeared in England about 1840, and its development was intended to provide a substitute for Derby "biscuit" porcelain which was then very expensive, and still is so today. Parian ware was made from a liquid clay, and formed by pouring into moulds. The resultant products were a fine grained, waxy feldspatic porcelain, resembling white parian marble.

Parian was developed in England by Copeland and Minton, and it gained considerable popularity when exhibited at the Crystal Palace during the 1851 Exhibition. It soon became a firm favourite in America for the production of parlour ornaments and busts. Bennington, who first introduced it to America, advertised it in 1852 as " figures in Parian Marble ", but the Americans varied the formula so much, that the examples produced may well be better described as " biscuit " porcelain, than parian. In Victorian England, the new material was an instant success. It provided means of giving miniature " sculptures " of classical style to a section of the community that otherwise would not have been able to afford such luxuries. Many early examples of statuettes were in fact, small reproductions of famous sculptures, but busts of famous people, nymphs, horses, small figures, plaques, vases, ornaments of great variety, and " useful " ware, in a type of waterproof parian, quickly followed. Although the majority of pieces are snowy white, parian will often be found tinted.

Plymouth

William Cookworthy (1705–1780), a Plymouth chemist, experimented for a number of years to produce a true hard porcelain, he was finally successful when he discovered the necessary raw materials in Cornwall. He patented his process in 1768, and started a factory at Coxside in Plymouth.

The majority of early wares were often slightly deformed and decorated in underglaze blue, with Chinese style and floral patterns. The enamelled wares were often decorated with flowers, and bird motifs. Figures, groups of figures, animal and bird models were included among the early examples.

The Plymouth factory only lasted two years. In 1770 Cookworthy removed to Bristol, and established a factory at Castle Green. This new factory was managed by a past associate, Richard Champion, who in 1773 purchased the business.

Under the control of Champion, the quality of the products were further improved. Figures of original design, and tablewares were skilfully made and decorated, but Plymouth porcelain was never really developed to a successful stage, competition from the many well established factories did not permit the necessary breathing space. In 1782, Champion sold the business.

Rockingham

The pottery at Swinton in Yorkshire was started about 1745 for the manufacture of earthenware, but much of the early examples were unmarked and cannot be identified with any real degree of certainty. Between 1778 and 1806 the pottery went through a phase of changing partnerships, but settled down in 1806 when two of the earlier partners, John and William Brameld, took over the business and operated under the title of " Brameld and Co ' using an impressed mark " Brameld ". William died in 1813 and his brother, Thomas, succeeded him.

By 1820 the pottery was a prosperous business with a considerable export trade, but in 1825 they were in serious financial trouble, which resulted in the firm becoming insolvent. The Marquess of Rockingham came to their aid by sponsoring a large sum of money. From this period the Marquess's crest, a griffin, and the name Rockingham was used as marks for " Rockingham " wares. It was about this time, the early 1820's, that examples in porcelain ware were first made. Rockingham porcelain has a soft, mellow, quality. Articles produced were the usual useful wares, animal models, figures, baskets, ornate vases and beautifully decorated dishes. Figures, groups, and busts were also produced in unglazed porcelain. Much of the finer pieces were superbly finished by expensive decorations.

However, once again, in 1842, the firm found itself in trouble and unable to compete with the more prosperous and commercially minded Staffordshire and Worcester potteries, and was finally forced to close.

Sèvres

Sèvres, the magic name in porcelain, that has almost become a standard reference for elegance, fine workmanship and original design. This French factory was established initially in an abandoned royal palace at Vincennes in 1738.

It was in a favoured position commercially, by virtue of having a monopoly protecting it from competition and giving it exclusive rights to manufacture porcelain. In 1753, it became a Royal factory and a factory mark incorporating the royal cypher was introduced and the title of the factory became " La Manufacture Royale de Porcelaine de France ".

In 1756 the factory was re-established at Sèvres. Three years later, in 1759, the King acquired a total interest in the Company.

The early examples produced at Vincennes were unmarked, they included ice pails, trays and simple forms. Very few figures were made since the pâté tendre, or soft paste, did not lend itself readily to moulding in the round or rococo style.

It was not until about 1769, when the necessary clay was found at Limoges, that hard paste porcelain was manufactured. Both hard and soft paste were used concurrently, but the hard paste products were marked with a crown and two crossed " L ", and named " Porcelaine Royale ".

The decorations of early Sèvres products were of an extremely high quality, including the many famous ground colours, of turquoise (bleu celeste), yellow (jaune jonquille), pea green, pink (rose pompadour), brilliant blue (bleu de roi).

These beautiful coloured grounds were applied leaving panels in which were painted figures, birds, and landscapes, framed in rich burnished gold.

Sèvres was famous also for its elaborately modelled flowers in porcelain, which were used to form decorative pieces on clocks, candelabra, and many other objects; sometimes they were included on porcelain figures.

Biscuit porcelain, as a material for figures, was used from about 1753. The work of E. M. Falconet, a sculptor who spent nine years at Sèvres, is among the best ever produced in the history of the factory.

In 1770 the Sèvres factory lost its monopoly, but it is still a flourishing Company to this day.

Spode

Josiah Spode (1733–97) was once employed by Whieldon. In 1770 he started the Spode Works, at Stoke-on-Trent, making earthenware, often decorated with blue printed patterns underglazed, in common with other manufacturers of the times. Excellent basalt ware was also produced which exhibited the fine quality and workmanship associated with Spode.

The majority of the examples of earthenware made from about 1790 had the mark impressed into the body or printed in blue. Josiah's son (1754–1827) who eventually carried on the pottery, added porcelain ware in about 1800 and he is considered to be the inventor of bone china, being the first to use bone ash in his porcelain. Bone China soon became popular and it is still considered to be the best quality porcelain today. Spode's products were always well potted, and of a high standard, well decorated and finished with skilful gilding. Up to 1822 Henry Daniel executed most of the enamel painting of Spode porcelain. Daniel later started his own works at Stoke and traded under the name of " Daniel & Son ".

In 1805 " Stone China " or " New Stone " was introduced as a cheap substitute for porcelain. Fine tableware was produced in this new material, decorated in patterns of Chinese origin, which were first outlined by means of transfer printing and subsequently coloured by hand. Josiah Spode, the second, died in 1827 and the firm was eventually taken over by the Copelands.

Staffordshire Pottery

Rare examples of Staffordshire pottery figures are now collectors pieces commanding high prices, but if we turn our attention to the less expensive " Staffordshire Figures " we enter a field of relatively inexpensive pottery. These figures were intended for the chimney pieces of cottages, not for the china-cabinets of the wealthy, but despite their lowly standing, they represent the sentiment of Victorian folk art, and as such can be fully appreciated.

Whilst the factories of Bow and Chelsea were looking to Europe for their inspiration for their figures, and concentrating on the well-to-do purchaser, the potters engaged on the coarse " image toys " as these small figures were named by Wedgwood, were looking at a much less lucrative market, and therefore could not afford to copy the European styles, instead they looked at life around them.

Many Staffordshire figures had " flat backs ", this means that the moulding of the figures was not continued at the back of the figure where it would not normally be seen. This was an obvious economy to save work on mould making and provided a shape suitable for resting on the chimney corners and mantles. The completely modelled figures such as Jenny Lind, Mrs Bloomer and similar examples are among the more expensive items.

Many firms were engaged in producing these figures and as the majority were situated in Staffordshire, it has become a general term to describe such wares, but they were also made in Liverpool, Leeds, Sunderland, Swansea and Scotland.

The names of such firms are relatively unimportant, and their work was rarely marked; however, Sampson Smith, James Dudson, and William Kent, were three of the better known makers who were engaged in making

French Poodles, Welsh Sheep Dogs, Spaniels, Grey-hounds, and many other items.

Early figures, which were modelled completely (no flat back) were better identified by marking. Ralph Wood Sewer (1715–1772) or Junior (1748–1795) made early Staffordshire figures in pottery to compete with the elegant porcelain of Chelsea and Derby and other factories, they were extremely fine examples, soft coloured, in yellow and green and blue, but unfortunately they are now very rare and expensive.

Thomas Whieldon (1719–1795) who once had Josiah Wedgwood as a junior partner, was another early master potter of note.

The most common Staffordshire item must surely be the Dogs, but figures of Robin Hood, Lord Byron, Soldier Boy, Flute Player, Richard the Third, Shakespeare, Will Watch, Emperor Napoleon, the Lion Slayer, Bag Pipe Player, Wellington, Equestrian Dick Turpin, and Tom King, Equestrian General MacDonald, Equestrian General Kitchener and Equestrian General Buller are just a few of the varied examples available in size from three to about nineteen inches high.

Miniature cottages, churches, summer houses, castles and animals were produced at the same time as the figures and for much the same market.

The miniature buildings were often designed for pastille burning, which was an aromatic substance burned for cleansing or scenting a room. The smoke issued from the tiny chimney in a most realistic manner, or through detachable perforated lids. There are also cottage money boxes.

There is obviously a great opportunity to specialise, if you can afford it—collect early figures and groups; if not—you can make a collection with a theme from any of the following: Animals, equestrian figures, military figures, theatrical figures, Royal figures, or even invent a category of your own choice.

Modern reproductions of some of the most desirable pieces were inevitable, and certain well known figures,

Left : Jasper, blue with applied yellow and white strapwork, applied flowers inside bowl, scroll and rope border on foot. 1790. Dia. 9½″.
Right: Oblong dish solid white Jasper, blue, yellow and white strapwork. 1790. 7½″.
(Josiah Wedgwood & Sons Ltd.)

such as Shakespearian characters, have been reproduced, often from original moulds. Recognition of such pieces is not difficult if you have handled sufficient " right " ones, look for glaze, colour, and the " feel " of the piece. Weight is not an important factor, some manufacturers seemed to have produced light figures, others preferred to make them heavier.

WEDGWOOD

Josiah Wedgwood, England's most famous master potter, was born in 1730. He was christened at Burslem on the 12th July, 1730, the youngest son of Thomas and

Mary Wedgwood of the Churchyard Pottery. Josiah was the twelfth child of this marriage.

Thomas Wedgwood, the father of Josiah, died in 1739, leaving the Churchyard Pottery to his eldest son Thomas. Josiah was then put to work in the family business under the control of his brother, and was apprenticed to him for a period of five years from November 11th, 1744. (The

Custard cup and cover, Queen's Ware, painted oak border, taken from pattern book of 1770, green and brown, typical of the graceful borders which emphasize the hard, smooth and even glaze of the ware. 1775. $3\frac{1}{2}''$.
Sugar box and cover, Queen's Ware, painted laurel border in brown, taken from Josiah Wedgwood's pattern book of 1770. 1780. $3''$.
Herring dish, Queen's Ware, centre design of embossed fish, handpainted border. 1779. $11''$.
Cream jug, Queen's Ware, painted strawberry leaf pattern, green, brown and gold, taken from Wedgwood's original pattern book of 1770. 1785. $3\frac{1}{2}''$.
(Josiah Wedgwood & Sons Ltd.)

Cup and saucer, Black Basalt, decorated in red and white encaustic
colours. 1778. Height 2½″.
Teapot, Black Basalt, thrown and engine turned, lion knob, top cut in
form of low parapet. 1780. Height 4½″.
(*Josiah Wedgwood & Sons Ltd.*)

indentures of his apprenticeship can be seen in the Hanley
Museum.)

On completion of his apprenticeship, Josiah left the
family business and went into partnership with a potter
named Harrison who had a works at Cliff Bank.

This partnership only lasted a few years, in 1754 he
entered into a partnership with Thomas Whieldon, of
Fenton, the most famous Staffordshire potter of the time,
who was noted for his technical skill and knowledge of
the trade. At this time Whieldon was making pottery of
outstanding quality including the mottled, agate and
marbled stonewares, and the black and coloured glazed
earthenwares.

Josiah Wedgwood's independent career can be said to have started from the early part of 1759, when at the age of 29, he left Whieldon and leased a part of his cousin's works, known as the Ivy House Pottery. Wedgwood was a ceaseless experimenter, and one of his many early inventions—the famous green glaze—was developed soon after his arrival at the Ivy House Potteries. This green glaze was used on many wares including covered sugar basins, and tea pots, often with gilded mottled sprigs.

About 1763, Wedgwood was producing a great variety of tableware and pottery known as ordinary " Dry Bodies ", that is pottery with its outer surfaces left

Left: Drinking mug, "Bringing Home the Game", Black Basalt, engine turned, silver mount, applied decoration, decorated handle, runner beads. Marked "Wedgwood". 1785. $3\frac{1}{2}''$.

Right: Drinking mug, Black Basalt, embossed beehive pattern. Marked "Wedgwood". 1830. $3\frac{1}{2}''$.

(Josiah Wedgwood & Sons Ltd.)

THE PORTLAND VASE

The most famous of all Jasper pieces is Wedgwood's replica of the Barberini or Portland Vase. This vase (now in the British Museum) was probably made about A.D. 50, possibly in Alexandria, by Greek glassmakers.

For many years the vase was in the possession of the Italian family of Barberini. In the 17th century it was purchased by Sir William Hamilton, a friend of Josiah Wedgwood, FRS. Sir William later sold it to the Duchess of Portland, whose son loaned it to Wedgwood.

The reproduction of the Portland Vase in Jasper is one of the ceramic achievements of all time. Wedgwood was highly praised for his skill by the famous people of the day.

Since 1878 the Portland Vase has been the registered trade mark of Josiah Wedgwood & Sons Ltd.

unglazed. A speciality of Wedgwood's Dry Bodies, was the red terra-cotta or Rosso Antico. Teapots were produced in terra-cotta with white stoneware reliefs, and punch kettles louped and mottled to imitate basket work. Terra-cotta pottery was not a new innovation of Wedgwood's but in his hands it took on a new freshness, elegance, and precision.

From the early 18th century, Staffordshire potters had been experimenting to obtain a white or light coloured earthenware, to compete with the tin enamelled faience produced in Europe and in oriental porcelains, so highly esteemed by the well to do. By about 1765 Wedgwood had perfected a cream ware for plates, dishes, tureens, sauceboats, cups and saucers, jugs, teapots and general tableware. This very practical, " useful ware " gained Wedgwood royal patronage, from then on this cream ware was known as " Queen's Ware ".

The black basalt, or black Egyptian, was used by Wedgwood for vases, candlesticks, busts, and many other ornamental objects. The material was a dense fine grain stoneware coloured by the addition of clay ironstone and magnesium ore. This mixture when fired produced a hard, dense stone capable of taking a high polish or engraving as would an agate or blood stone.

Vases and similar articles were often decorated by Wedgwood in encaustic colours. This was a process by which gold was attached to the surface of the black basalt or other dry bodies using japanner's size as an adhesive. Examples of this type of decoration are now rare, the gold most probably having been worn away with the passage of time. In 1768 Wedgwood was introduced to a merchant named Thomas Bently. Bently was a well educated man, much travelled, and very much interested in the revival of classic styles. The interest in these styles no doubt largely resulting from the works of art found in the diggings of Pompeii and Herculaneum. Wedgwood and Bently became firm friends, and business partners. They built a new pottery just outside Burslem, a house for the master, and an entire village for the workers. This village was named Etruria. The pottery operated until about 1950, when it was removed to Barlaston, just outside Stoke.

About this time Wedgwood was producing cane coloured pie dishes in several sizes and generally ornamented with modelled leaves and berries. Other examples were made without ornamentation except those with crimped edge resembling the rim of a pie.

It is for his Jasper ware that Wedgwood is best known. Examples of this beautiful " Wedgwood Blue " had been produced over the past 200 years and are appreciated by both collector and admirer all over the world.

Josiah Wedgwood required a white stone ware of infinite fineness, capable of being tinted, and hard enough to be polished, so that he could manufacture the reproductions of the " Greco-Roman " gems of polish stone or coloured glass. He experimented with every kind of likely white material that he could obtain. About 1773 and 1774 he tried hundreds of different combinations using different clays and earths in an endeavour to perfect the whiteness, and reliability during firing, of the glossy white stone ware, or white porcelain bisket. Wedgwood's tenacity was eventually rewarded, the answer lay in a sulphate of berrium associated with lead ore mined in Derbyshire. By 1775 he was producing a fine white terracotta. This was a material with a smooth waxy surface, on which cameos were made in relief and closely resembled ivory carvings. The ground was often coloured by hand. It was not, however, the Jasper ware that we know today, this was to come a little later with a mixture of sulphate of berrium 59 parts; clay 29 parts; flint 10 parts; and carbonate of berrium 2 parts. Wedgwood found that this porcelain-like material could be uniformally stained by using the ordinary mineral oxides which were generally used in colouring pottery to the various tones of lilac, blue, green and yellow as well as to an intense black. Wedgwood's Jasper was now an accomplished fact.

Although Wedgwood blue ground colour may be the most common it was produced in a number of other distinct tints, each of which may occur in several different shades. Ground colours vary from a dark, almost indigo, blue through several distinct shades to a pale lavender blue, there are several shades of sage green, and an olive green which ranges from a dark to a lighter shade, this latter colouration is more rare. One other green tending towards blue was also used. The black of Jasper ware was a deep, rich, full black and was used extensively for the reproduction of model figures and busts. It was also used in the production of decorated vases, these beautiful examples had the black body decorated with relief in white Jasper.

Bently died in November 1780, and was buried at Chiswick on December 2nd, 1780. With the loss of Bently Josiah Wedgwood carried on the business on his own account for a year and then, on January 18th, 1790 Wedgwood's three sons John, Josiah and Thomas and his nephew Thomas Byreley were taken into partnership. The title of the Company now became " Josiah Wedgwood, Sons and Byreley."

Wedgwoods most famous antique reproduction is undoubtedly the Portland Vase the original of this vase was a Greco-Roman work in glass found in a sepulchre mound a few miles outside of Rome. The vase was enshrined in a marble sarcophagus. The Duke of Portland bought the vase after his wife's death in 1785, and loaned it to Wedgwood so that he could copy it. Examples of the Wedgwood reproduction of the Portland Vase can be seen in the British Museum and Victoria and Albert Museum.

One of the most eventful and exciting chapters in the history of Wedgwood came to a close on January 3rd, 1795 when Josiah Wedgwood died. It was, however, only the end of a chapter and not the end of the story, the descendants of Wedgwood are maintaining their high standard synonymous with Wedgwood in their new factory at Barlaston.

Jasper Ware

The Jasper ware so beloved by the collector, owes its appeal mainly to the relief decoration. These decorations are still made today in much the same way that Wedgwood made them nearly 200 years ago. The beautiful little reliefs, irrespective of their design, were first produced in oak moulds. These moulds had the designs in intaglio, that is, the design was sunken below the surface. Clay of the same composition as the piece to which the decoration was to be added, was then formed by pressing into the mould. The clay moulding was then carefully removed from the mould and applied to the surface of the article by moistening with water. Both the clay of the moulding and the article were at this stage a slaty grey, it was only during the firing process that the colouring oxides became effective, the stained ground taking on one of the famous colours, and the relief becoming outstandingly white.

The high quality of Wedgwood's early reliefs were obtained by further handwork after they left the mould. The moulds had to be designed in such a way that the clay pressed into them could be removed easily, therefore, it was not possible to have any undercutting, where these were required, skilled workmen were employed to hand finish, by accentuating certain lines, and rounding off projections, otherwise not possible from a one piece mould.

The quality of undercutting and finishing is one of the tests for early pieces.

Tableware

Jasper ware tea and coffee sets were produced by Wedgwood with the same degree of attention that was lavished on all his work. It is unlikely that a new collector will be able to buy a complete, early tea or coffee set even if he had the money, such is the demand today for early Wedgwood. Tea and coffee pots could form the basis of the original collection, and then other pieces added as the opportunity arises. Even an odd cup in Jasper ware is an object of beauty and will not look out of place

SCENT BOTTLE
Cut glass with Jasper medallion, white on black, designed by Lady Templeton. 1785. Height 2¾″.

PIN BOX
Upright octagonal, with blue and white cameo inset in lid, mounted with cut steal band surround. Pale green velvet pincushion with 18th century hand made pins inside. 1786.

OPERA GLASS
Single telescopic lens mounted in ivory and ormolu, tube of Jasper, white on blue with subjects modelled by Hackwood from the Marlborough Gem, "Marriage of Cupid and Psyche" and "Sacrifice to Hymen". Height 3″.

(Josiah Wedgwood & Sons Ltd.)

among your other items of Wedgwood because the saucer is missing. There are many types of Jasper jugs ranging from fairly squat, rotund vessels to the severely upright with, or without covered tops. Your tableware collection can be extended with tea caddies, preserve jars, butter luggers, sugar bowls and not forgetting the biscuit barrel. All these items of tableware have been made in the typical blue and green jasper colours decorated with the white jasper reliefs.

Small Boxes, etc.

There are a considerable number of little boxes that were originally designed for the toilet table. Oblong boxes were made completely in Jasper ware, and in other materials such as ivory and wood with inset cameos of Jasper. Dainty and attractive powder boxes were made in tortoise shell and inlaid with Jasper cameos.

Scent or smelling bottles can be obtained in numerous shapes and sizes, and in every colour of Jasper ware. More unusual scent bottles were made in cut glass, with cameos or medallions set into the sides. The more exotic examples had a cameo on each side of the cut glass bottle. Small Jasper ware cameos have always been popular in

Early Morning Teaset, five pieces, teapot with cover, sugar box with cover, cream jug, cup and saucer and tray, "Domestic Employment", designed by Lady Templeton and modelled by William Hackwood in 1783. Jasper, white on blue, thrown and turned. 1784. Height of Teapot 4″
(*Josiah Wedgwood & Sons Ltd.*)

jewellery. They have been made into brooches, clasps, buckles, and lockets hung from a chain around the neck. Other collectable items of jewellery will include cameo rings, scarf and hat pins, cloak and hair pins.

Plaques

Jasper ware plaques are interesting collectors items. They will often be seen framed and hanging on walls, or in collectors cabinets. These plaques were not intended as an end product in themselves, but were in fact, ornamental pieces designed as furniture fittings. These plaques, either round, oval or rectangular, were used either singly or in combination for fireplace surrounds, window shutter decorations, inset into chests of drawers, cabinets, book cases, tables, clocks and ink stands. This is by no means an extensive list of the uses found for this most versatile and attractive form of applied decoration.

Vases

Vases, urns, and bowls were Wedgwood's pride and joy and are probably sought after by collectors more than any other item of Jasper ware. Very early vases and urns will be well out of the reach of a new collector, they will already be in the possession of a Museum, or a wealthy collector. However it still may be possible to obtain relatively late examples.

Worcester

Although the Worcester factory was founded in 1751, it is unlikely that anything was produced until 1752, when the Bristol factory was acquired. Dr John Wall, a well known physician, became an important partner, and the period 1751 to 1783 became known as the " Dr. Wall Period ". The administration of the actual pottery was under the control of William Davis, another partner. The manufacture of Worcester porcelain incorporated soapstone in the formula, and during the Dr. Wall period, the porcelain was greyish in colour, but had a greenish tint when viewed by transmitted light. The glaze was a hard thin coating that had a tendency to shrink away from the

Worcester Jug "May Day" design on glaze, printed and tinted.
(*Worcester Royal Porcelain Co. Ltd.*)

Worcester Vase and Cover, painted with onglaze "dry blue" colours.
Worcester first period C. 1765.
(Worcester Royal Porcelain Co. Ltd.)

Worcester plate and bowl with "pencilled" decoration in the "Jesuit" style. (*Worcester Royal Porcelain Co. Ltd.*)

Worcester plate, part of the Lady Mary Worthley Montague service, with ground in scale blue.
(*Worcester Royal Porcelain Co. Ltd.*)

foot rim of cups, plates, and similar articles, which left a dry, unglazed, ring where it had shrunk away.

Early pieces of Worcester were almost indistinguishable from the Bristol examples, including the decoration in underglaze blue, and the more elaborate examples painted in polychrome enamels, depicting Chinese figures with flower and animal backgrounds.

By about 1760, the pottery was producing examples decorated with European figure and landscape subjects executed in a fine, black, line. Transfer printing over the glaze was a technique much used from about 1756, incorporating black, lilac, and a brick red colouring. By 1770 the decoration of Worcestor porcelain became more elaborate, and more like Sévres in style. No doubt, this work was probably executed by Chelsea artists who moved to Worcester at that time.

Vases, bowls, and other suitable wares, decorated with beautifully coloured backgrounds, surrounded inset panels, with figures and exotic birds. The most common background colour was an underglaze blue, a popular variation of which was known as " Scale Blue ". The effect was obtained by painting or " Wiping out " the coloured areas to simulate the scales on a fish. The scale designs were used with overglazed colours in yellow, pink, red and purple, but these are very rare.

Plain, rich coloured grounds painted in sky blue, pink, purple and apple green are also rare. A peculiarity of the apple green was its rejection of gilding, so gilt decorations were always added in close proximity of the ground colour and not over it.

Only a few figure and animal pieces were made, but these also are extremely rare.

In 1783, the " Dr. Wall Period " ended, and the firm was sold to Thomas Flight. New designs in neo-classic styles were introduced, with fluted forms and Grecian motifs. The central medallion with inset pictures of classical figures and landscapes were much featured.

Flight had purchased the Company for his two sons, when one died in 1791 the surviving brother went into partnership with Martin Barr, and the Company became known as " Flight and Barr ". Various other changes in partnerships and combines finally resulted in the forming of the Royal Worcester Porcelain Company, in 1862, which is still operating today.

GLOSSARY

Agate Ware: Wares made to imitate the agate. The effect was obtained by mixing different coloured clays, in which case the colours go right through the body. Another means of achieving the same result was to apply coloured clays on the surface of otherwise plain pottery.

Bamboo-Ware: A type of stoneware similar to the caneware invented by Josiah Wedgwood, but slightly darker in tint.

Basalts: Fine quality black stoneware made famous by Josiah Wedgwood.

Bellarmine: Large stoneware bottle named after Cardinal Bellarmine. Decorated with a bearded mask in relief.

Bisket: Unglazed porcelain.

Black Egyptian: An unglazed black stoneware, Wedgwood's basalts.

Bocage: A flower and foliage background, usually associated with figures and groups.

Body: The potters clay, the material from which pottery or stoneware is made.

Bone China: So named because white ashes of bone were used in this type of porcelain.

Cane-Ware: Fine unglazed buff stoneware.

" Cauliflower-Ware ": Glazed earthenware often in the form of cauliflowers and pineapples etc., coloured green and yellow. One of Wedgwood's products.

Celadon Wares: Wares with felspathic glaze of a pale grey or blue green tone.

China-Clay: Fine porcelain clay chiefly produced from feldspar, also known as kaolin.

China-Stones: A crystallised mineral comprising silicates of aluminium with varying proportions of pot ash, lime or soda, decomposed granite, used with china clay to produce porcelain.

Chinoiserie: Exotic and elaborate decoration depicting Chinese figures, encompassed by flowers, birds and animals, often highly coloured, including gold and silver.

Cloisonné Ware: Enamel metal on which the design is made by thin metal strips. The enamelled colours are contained within.

Combed Slip: Marbled or feathered effect obtained by brushing together two or more different coloured wet slips.

Crazing: Reticulation of the glaze causing minute cracks to appear on the surface. Caused by differential shrinkage of body and glaze.

Creamware: A lead glaze earthenware made of pale coloured clay usually containing calcined flint.

Enamel: A means of decorating porcelain in vitreous colours, which fuse upon the glazed surface. On soft paste porcelain the enamels are absorbed into the fusible lead glaze but on hard paste porcelain this does not occur.

Victorian Moustache Cup in decorated porcelain. Internal lip prevented long moustaches from getting wet whilst drinking.
(*D. C. Gohm*)

Encaustic Painting: An ancient style of decorative art consisting in painting on heated wax. Wedgwood was granted a patent in 1769 for a very similar process involving the decoration of porcelain with encaustic gold bands. It was used by him to decorate some of his early wares in imitation of ancient Greek ware.

Faience: A loosely applied term for all kinds of white pottery.

Famille Rose: A class of enamelled wares characteristic of the reigns of Yung Cheng and Ch'ien Lung named after the rose colour introduced from Europe.

Feldspathic Glazes: Glazes containing feldspar.

Glaze: There are many types of glazes, but they are all designed to impart a shiny coating to porcelain which makes them proof against liquids. Glazes can be made opaque, coloured or translucent, depending upon their purpose.

Hard Paste: The component materials of porcelain are china clay and china stone. Presenting a very hard porcelain when glazed.

Imari: Japanese porcelain decorated in underglaze iron red, blue and gold. The name is derived from a Port in Japan of the same name.

Impasto: A thick application of colour which makes the design stand out away from the ground.

Jasper-Ware: A fine grain unglazed stoneware perfected by Wedgwood. (See text.)

Majolica: A 19th century English name used to describe lead-glazed pottery of 16th century French style. (See Delftware.)

Marble Ware: See Agate ware.

Moucha Ware: Made from about 1775 until 1914, the name was derived from Moucha Quartz. A form of decoration with coloured bands into which fern like motifs have been superimposed.

Parian: A marble like feldspathic porcelain. (See text.)

Porcelain: The finest kind of earthenware—white glazed and semi transulcent.

Pottery: Usually refers to earthenwares fired at low temperatures. Stoneware and porcelain require very high temperatures by comparison.

Red Ware: Made of red clay pottery.

Registry Mark: See tables at end of book.

Salt-glazed Stoneware: A method of glazing stoneware by throwing common salt into the kiln when it reaches its highest temperature.

Slip: Clay reduced by water to a creamy consistency. Normally used to form decorations or to completely coat with another colour. (See Combed slip.)

Soft-Paste: A porcelain made from white clay and soap stone, bone ash or some other material. Not a true porcelain.

Tin Glaze: Basically a lead glaze that has been made opaque by adding tin ashes.

Underglaze Decorations: As the name implies the decoration was applied before glazing.

POT LIDS

The idea of product marketing by using attractive packaging is not a new one. The 19th century had its share of " marketing managers ", and these have provided an item for modern collectors, namely the pot lid.

The jars for which the pot lids were designed were made to contain a variety of substances, such as meat pastes, pickles, pomades, creams, bear grease, and a host of other such products.

Between 1830 and 1840 a considerable number of different types of pots were being made, and decorated by hand painting, or single colour printed patterns. Earthenware lids were produced a little later, by using a multi-colour print, which was applied by a mechanical process, under the glaze.

The printed pattern was applied by transferring each colour from separately engraved plates by the use of transfer paper. This was a very skilful operation, requiring each transfer to be accurately superimposed on the impression previously printed. As an aid to this operation, registration dots, or small circles, were printed on each side of the decoration. Most pot lids carry these marks.

Pot lids are generally known as " Pratt " after the Staffordshire pottery firm of F. & R. Pratt, and it was this firm that produced the majority of these items. In 1847 Felix Pratt took out a patent which " productionised " his pot manufacture. This invention took the form of a double gauge to be used in conjunction with the throwing wheel, and it is presumed that the gauges were used to form both the inner and outer surfaces of the pot.

Many pot lids owe their attractiveness to the skill of Jessie Austin, artist and engraver, and a one time employee of Pratt. His signature will appear on many of the best examples of multi-coloured printed patterns.

There are a great number of different types of pot lids, and it is suggested that the collector should initially con-

Pot Lid. 5¼″ dia. "The Grand International Building of 1851".
(*Loco Antiques*)

centrate his efforts to items contained in a specific category. Suggested categories are figures, portraits, landscapes, animals and birds, flower subjects, historical pictures, or lids carrying the name of the vendor, or even naming the contents.

Collectors are not usually recommended to accept damaged or faulty examples, irrespective of the price at which these are offered.

Potential pot lid collectors should refer to H. G. Clark's " The Pictorial Pot Lid Book." An edition was published in 1960, which describes many types.

PRINTS

Of all the subjects that can be formed into a collection, antique prints must be the most rewarding. They can be stored in portfolios which take very little space, the best can be framed and displayed, their range is inexhaustible, and they can be bought at prices to suit practically every pocket.

Early prints were made from woodcuts, and although these have much to commend them, they are only sought after usually by specialist collectors. We will, therefore, concentrate our attention on the generally more desirable types of engravings.

It will be useful, and increase our appreciation of prints, if we learn something about the style and methods used by early engravers to produce the fine examples of their craft, and to be able to readily recognise these styles when examining prints with a view to acquisition.

Line Engraving

The plate used for a line engraving was usually copper, other materials have been used but not to the same extent. On this sheet the engraver traced the outline of the subject to be engraved, then, with a burin or graver, held in the hand, proceeded to follow the traced outline, cutting a groove into the plate. By varying the width and depth of the groove the engraver controlled the amount of ink that could be held, this resulted in either a coarse or fine line on the printed impression.

As far as it is known, the earliest engraving on copper was in 1545. Later engravings on steel, recognised by the overall fineness of line, were made from about 1820 or later.

Lithographs

Lithographs were produced by drawing the subject on a specially prepared stone. The piece of stone, usually a limestone, was first given a granular surface and flattened by rubbing with another piece of similar stone. For the drawing, a greasy chalk was used. The stone was

F

then subjected to the action of a weak acid and prints obtained by wetting the surface of the stone with water, and then applying the ink with a roller. The ink, being of a greasy nature, adhered to the greasy drawing, but was rejected by the water over the remainder of the stone. A piece of damp paper was finally pressed onto the stone, and the image transferred.

It is unlikely that you will find any lithographs earlier than the early part of the 19th century, although the process was discovered in 1796.

Lithographs are recognised by their approximation to pencil drawings.

Mezzotint

The copper plate used for mezzotints was first prepared by polishing, then, with chalk, parallel lines were drawn across the plate, about $\frac{3}{4}$ inch apart. The engraver then took a curved tool with one edge grooved and sharpened to form a series of dots and, placing this tool between the first two chalk lines, rocked it back and forth, slowly moving across the plate. This action produced a band of zig-zag indentations in the plate. He then proceeded across the second chalk line, and so on until the whole surface had been evenly roughened. operation was repeated diagonally and at various angles until the whole surface had been evenly roughened.

At this stage, if the plate was inked and an impression taken, the result would be an even black, velvety rectangle.

The actual subject was developed by scraping away areas of the roughened plate and polishing to obtain the variety of tones.

This process has been used for various subjects, but it is most commonly found in portraiture.

Mezzotints date from about the middle of the 17th century.

Aquatint

Aquatints were produced by scattering finely powdered resin evenly over a copper plate, and then heating just sufficiently to melt the resin, and so fix it to the plate. The method of distributing the resin was to place the plate in a wooden box and rotate it, by a fan inside the box, or by simply blowing with a bellows.

Another method was to cover the plate with a solution of resin and spirits of wine. The evaporation of the spirit left the resin as a dry thin film.

Whichever method of resin application was used, the result was the same—a multitude of separate grains caused by the contraction of the resin on drying, and exposing the raw copper in between the grains.

The picture was then developed by the application of acid on top of the resinous ground, the acid biting into the plate in the exposed areas only. The graduations of tone were obtained by successive bitings with acid, and stopping out with an acid resistant varnish.

Aquatints date approximately from the middle of the 18th century, and can be recognised by examination of the darker passages which will show the granulated texture typical of the method.

Stipple

The engraver first covered a copper plate with a film of wax, then with the aid of an etching needle, proceeded to outline the subject by pricking dots through the wax to expose the metal underneath. The darker passages were then treated with larger dots, or by closer groupings, and then the plate bitten by acid. The etchings ground was then removed, and the acid bitten dots re-worked with a curved graver, known as a stipple graver.

Skilfully executed stipple engravings are very beautiful and are recognised by the obvious dot construction.

Various methods of producing stipple were used as early as 1589, but the type described above will mainly interest the collector and these date from the latter half of the 18th century.

Dry Point

Dry point engravings were made by a very simple process. The subject was engraved into the copper plate with a needle which left a burr on each edge of the line. This burr held the ink as well as the engraved groove, and so produced a rich line.

Because the raised burr was easily damaged and wore away quickly during printing, it was not possible to get any great quantities of good impressions, therefore they will be difficult to find in good condition.

Dry point engravings date from about the middle of the 17th century.

Etchings

This was the simplest of all the methods—a copper plate was covered with a wax ground and the subject drawn with a needle to expose the copper. Acid was then applied which bit into the plate along the lines traced by the needle. When the lighter weight lines reached the required depth, the plate was removed from the acid and these " stopped " by the application of an acid resistant varnish.

By successive applications of varnish and acid dips, lines could be produced varying from the very fine to the darkest.

The etching process is believed to have been used by mediaeval goldsmiths but it was not until the early part of the 16th century that it was used to create prints.

Soft Ground Etchings

A wax ground was laid over a copper plate, and then covered by a thin sheet of paper. The engraver, or artist, then drew the subject on the paper with a pencil, varying the line thickness by varying the pressure on the pencil. When the paper was removed, the wax adhered to the drawn image, and so exposed the copper for acid biting.

Soft ground etchings resemble crayon drawings and date from the early 19th century.

General Notes

Often the word " state " is used when referring to prints, and refers simply to the different stages through which a print passes. Proofs taken by the engraver during the process to check his work should not be considered a " state ". The state became meaningful only after the plate is complete, this would constitute a first state; the addition of any text or title would be a second state; and should the plate be returned to the engraver for any repair work, the resulting impression would be considered a further state, and so on.

The majority of prints were engraved by skilled engravers from originals by well known artists, but not always, some artists preferred to engrave their own work if they had the ability. The name of the artist and the engraver are more often than not indicated somewhere on the print, usually along the bottom of the impression, one on the left side, the other on the right.

Good quality prints, irrespective of the techniques employed, should have adequate margins surrounding the actual picture and title; no part of the picture, text, or name of publisher should be cut, or removed. Ideally the original margins should be intact, but these are the rarity rather than the rule.

The actual subject, that is the complete ink impression, should be clean and well defined. Prints made from worn plates will be obvious by the lack of definitions in certain areas, and retouched plates tend to stand out boldly in the areas reworked.

If a print should have a slight tear, or one that has been well repaired, do not discard it as a worthless item, its value will certainly be less than that of a perfect specimen, but it may be almost impossible to obtain that particular print in excellent condition. If you should find a better specimen at a later date, replace it, and sell the damaged print. Beware of prints that have been laid down, that is pasted to another sheet of paper or a backing board, this is often done to hold a badly damaged print together. It should be possible to hold the print up against the light for examination of any possible repairs or watermarks.

The quality of the paper is important, but this can only be assessed after the experience of examining and handling many prints.

Paper of the 18th century is generally soft with a texture not unlike blotting paper, but later papers tend to have stronger, harsher feel.

One point in respect of paper—some very fine prints were produced on India paper, which is tissue thin and then pasted to a backing. This type of printing was a standard method and in no way detracts from the value.

Apart from the antique prints that were printed in colour by such artists as Le Blon and Bartolozzi, the printed tints on lithographs, and some coloured stipple engravings, the vast majority of prints were hand coloured using water-colours. It is obviously much better to collect prints that were contemporary coloured but so many prints offered for sale today have been subjected to the attention of modern amateur colourists and bear no resemblance to the old style. There are, however, a few professional restorers of prints with the ability and knowledge to apply the paint in such a manner that the result is contemporary of the period.

Where possible collect prints with the original colour, or those restored by skilled colourists, and so maintain a standard of quality.

Whilst on the subject of restoration—if you should find a print that is discoloured, or foxed, or has faded colours, do not reject it on account of these apparent defects, a print restorer will clean the print and remove the fox marks quite cheaply.

The demand for antique prints is such that it has become increasingly difficult to find a large enough supply. High prices are paid for old books containing engravings, which are then broken and sold individually, and there has been considerable increase in the sale of reproductions. These reproductions have no real value and should never be considered by a serious collector.

It is difficult to give any real indication of value, mainly because the variety is so tremendous, and like every commodity, the question of supply and demand, quality, rarity, and condition has a great influence on the asking price, but tread warily, begin your collection with prints costing only shillings, the higher priced engravings can wait until sufficient knowledge of the subject has been gained.

Well known dealers in prints issue a catalogue and these can be used as a guide to current prices. Prints obtained at sales, junk shops, and the odd antique dealer should be well below the specialist dealer price.

What to collect? The answer to this question can only really be determined by the collector himself, it largely depends on his personal taste and means.

You can choose a subject, or subjects, artist, or engraver, or even styles of engraving. The following suggestions are by no means comprehensive, but are offered as a stepping stone to a deeper understanding.

Marine

Good quality marine prints of clippers, yachts, and shipping generally, are in great demand and consequently command high prices. Sea battles offer a reasonable alternative, these are not quite so expensive, but usually the ships are in exquisite detail.

T. G. Dutton; W. J. Huggins; W. Daniell; and E. W. Cooke are just a few of the best known marine artists.

Sporting

There is a tremendous range of prints covered by this heading, almost every aspect of sport including hunting, fishing, shooting, archery, deer stalking, cycling and card games are well represented.

A few of the most prominent artists and engravers of sporting subjects are shown below as a general guide.

S. Alken.	1750–1825	Aquatint engraver. Good representative of equestrian art of his day.
H. Alken.	1784–1851	Very prolific sporting artist, also illustrator of many books.
H. B. Chalon.	1770–1849	Mainly a racing artist, but engraved a few dogs.

C. C. Henderson.	1803–1877	Some of the best coaching prints were produced after this artist.
J. F. Herring.	1795–1865	This artist produced very fine horse paintings, many of which were aquatinted by C. Hunt, a combination that gave us some wonderful prints.
G. Morland.	1763–1804	This artist covered many sporting subjects.
J. Pollard.	1797	A must in any collection of sporting prints, also well known for coaching subjects.
G. Stubbs.	1724–1806	One of the racing and horse artists.

Topographical

The potential print collector could not do better than gain his experience with topographical subjects. The choice is wide, prices for average quality prints reasonable, and every technique is represented.

The exquisite lithographs of London by T. S. Boys will be very expensive, but the post card size prints by Shepperd, extracted from his book, can be obtained for shillings.

Decorative

These prints are not too popular with collectors because they do not have any real historic appeal. The famous " Cries of London " after Wheatly, would be considered a decorative series.

George Baxter

George Baxter was born in 1804 and died in 1867. He was renowned for his beautiful oil colour prints, which were eagerly sought a few years ago. Of recent years they seem to have lost some of their popularity, but you will still find them relatively scarce, though not too expensive.

The prints were produced either on a mezzotint or aquatint base, and the colour tint added by means of separate blocks for each tint. It will be appreciated that considerable mechanical skill was required to register accurately a number of blocks.

Baxter prints will be found illustrating many books between the 1840's and 1850's, and it has been assumed that his illustrations for " The Feathered Tribes " in 1834 was his first such work.

Some of his best work includes " The Ascension " and " Descent from the Cross ". He also produced land-scapes, flower pictures, portraits, Sunday School cards, tiny pictures for needlework box decoration and so on. It is estimated that this prolific maker of prints produced over 400 different works, and if we consider the minute variations due to minor errors in manipulating the blocks, the total must well exceed several thousand variations.

A few points to note when acquiring. Like all prints, the margins should be good and the face unfaded. The name and address of Baxter should appear at the bottom of the impression, either in white or stamped on the margin or mounted in red. Incidentally Baxter had four different addresses during the period of his print-producing days.

Baxter licensed his process to other printers from about 1849, the best known of these were J. M. Kronheim, William Dickes, Bradshaw and Blacklock, Joseph Mansell and Le Blond. Le Blond in his early days used Baxter's name, but later reverted to his own.

Although not of the same quality of Baxter, the Le Blond " Ovals " are very attractive little prints and certainly worth collecting.

GLOSSARY

After: Refers to "after the design of a painter" — not an original work. The engravers would have copied a painting by another artist. For example "By G. Hunt after M. Egerton." If the engraver was also the artist, it would be stated "by and after G. Hunt".

Aquatint: A method of engraving. (See full process under sub-heading in text.)

Burin: An engraving tool.

Burnisher: A tool used to flatten the ground and so provide a high tone or soften a harsh line.

Burr: The rough edge formed along the engraved line by the engraving tool.

Counter Proof: A proof not taken direct from the plate, but off a print that had just been removed. Consequently counter proofs are reversed.

Dry Point: A method of engraving. (See full process under sub-heading in text.)

Etching: A method of engraving. (See full process under sub-heading in text.)

Foxed: Spotted brownish marks usually caused by damp.

Ground: The prepared surface of the plate, a preliminary stage before actual engraving is started, i.e. wax coating preparatory to etching.

India Paper: A very thin silky paper, absorbs ink to a greater extent than ordinary papers.

Laying Down: Prints pasted to paper, cardboard, or canvas, are said to be "laid down".

Line Engraving: A method of engraving. (See full process under sub-heading in text.)

Lithograph: A method of engraving. (See full process under separate heading in text.)

Mezzotint: A method of engraving. (Se full process under separate heading in text.)

Plate: The sheet of metal into which the design is engraved.

Plate Mark: The impression made by the edge of the plate on the paper during the printing process.

Proof: An impression taken from an engraved plate to check progress of the engraving.

Proof Before Letters: A proof taken before the title has been added.

State: A stage in the evolution of a print.

SEALED BOTTLES AND DECANTERS

During the 17th century, there were not the wine shops displaying a choice of attractively arrayed bottles as we know them today. Wine was transported from the Continent in casks, and the purchaser bought them in the same container.

To bring the wine to the table, it was necessary to use something more suitable, such as a bottle or decanter.

Early decanters were nothing more than a bottle with a stopper of cork or pewter, and well to do folk had bottles made with their own seal moulded on the surface for identification purposes. It is possible that such bottles were sent to the importers for refilling. These early " sealed bottles " have now become popular as a collectors item, and are becoming increasingly difficult to acquire. The type of bottle described as " onion " is English, and has a large round bulbous body, with a short thick neck. Shaft and globe describes a more elegant " onion ", it has a larger and thinner neck and the body is less squat. The " shaft and globe " developed in four main stages from the early 17th century to about 1740. Stage one, from 1620–60, they had bulbous bodies, long necks, flat lips, a string ring about $\frac{1}{2}''$ below the lip, and a low kick (a kick is the domed indentation seen in the base of the bottles, necessary to early bottle-making). Stage two, from about 1650 to 1685, the angle of the shoulder became more acute, and the body more tapering towards the base. Stage three, from 1680 to 1715, the body widened, and became more dumpy, the neck more tapering and shorter and the kick was quite high. Stage four, from about 1710 to 1740, body more square to the base, or with a tendency to an outward slant, with a well defined shoulder at the base of the neck.

From about 1730, the " shaft and globe " bottles were superseded by the more conventional cylindrical type.

George Ravenscroft (1618–81) is a famous name in

glass, in 1674 he took out a patent for making flint glass. The Glass-Sellers Company were so impressed with this new product, they agreed to take his total output, providing he adopted their standard designs.

From sealed bottles to decanters is an almost indefinable step. Decanters are still basically bottles, but they have a better sense of design and purpose. The " shaft and globe " shape was popular for clear glass decanters, and is still being used in modern designs.

From about 1750 we find decanters engraved, gilded or enamelled, with the name of the intended contents, such as Gin, Cherry, Rum, Brandy, Whiskey and of course Wine.

Bristol blue decanters, as their name suggests, were made at Bristol, from dark blue glass. They were decorated in gold, with the pattern of a wine label suspended from the neck. This type of decanter is rare, if however you are fortunate, and procure such a piece, you may find it signed by the maker—Isaac Jacobs. If no signature is found, it will almost be impossible to define its origin, as other makers copied the design and need not necessarily have come from Bristol.

From about 1765 to 1800, the decanter became more tapered with a less pronounced connection between body and neck. One of these varieties was shaped like an Indian Club and had vertical lines and horizontal hoops cut into its surface.

Closely following this period we find the Prussian type, with fluting halfway up the body. These may have been added to give an additional surface area to facilitate the cooling of the contents.

A considerable contribution was made by Irish and Scandinavian manufacturers, Waterford manufacturers produced many popular Prussian types. At the end of the 18th century we find rings appearing on the necks to prevent the vessel falling out of the hands. Belfast manufacturers appear to have preferred only two rings, instead of the more conventional three rings.

Decanter stoppers were rarely finished by grinding until after 1745, but from this date onwards, it was commonplace.

Stoppers were made to suit individual decanters, therefore it will be difficult to replace one that has become lost or broken.

When buying a decanter, check the stopper, make certain it fits properly, and that it is the correct type. You will find many specimens offered by sale with ill fitting or replacement stoppers.

Stoppers can be an interesting subject in their own right, and they are often offered for sale without decanters.

SHEFFIELD PLATE

Sheffield plate is a thin, but very permanent coating of sterling silver on copper. The coating process was not effected by any electro-chemical process but by fusing the two metals together under heat, without any amalgamation of the metals taking place. This resulted in a material that could be rolled and formed into a thin sheet from which the famous Sheffield Plate was subsequently manufactured. Unfortunately the process has now been lost, and superseded by the more modern plating methods.

Sheffield Plate was invented as a means of providing silverware much cheaper than the solid silver of the day, but as antiques go, its life span was a short one. From about 1760 to about 1850, eventually the even cheaper techniques of electro-plating ruined the industry.

Good Sheffield Plate compares very well with solid silver. The methods employed by the manufacturers were obviously copied from the silversmiths, even so, the platemakers difficulties, must have been enormous when they first soldered, raised and chased the silver faced copper into representations of solid silver. However they managed to do so, and produced a vast quantity and variety of pieces that lost nothing by comparison to the real silver pieces.

In 1743, Thomas Bolsover, a Sheffield cutler, made the discovery that silver could be fused to copper; his earliest experiments produced small boxes and buttons only.

In 1760, Matthew Boulton of Birmingham, began to manufacture from this new material and became one of the great names of the day.

In the 1760's it was not unusual to silver only one side of the copper, so it is possible to find an early vessel silvered on the exterior and only tinned on the interior. Similarly, a cooking pan could be silvered on the interior surface only.

Articles likely to corrode from the chemical actions of their contents were often gilded on the inside as a protection. Such items as salt-cellars, mustard pots and jugs will be found treated in this manner, rarely was the outside surfaces gilded.

Unlike silver, Sheffield Plate is not all hall-marked, prior to 1784 it was illegal to do so. From 1784, however, it was permissible for platers to put some identification such as their name or identifying mark on their products.

When prospecting for Sheffield Plate, inspect carefully, look at the joints and seams with a glass. If you cannot find any seams, or joints, they have probably been covered up by electro-plating and you can conclude that it is not a genuine old piece.

Although the coating of silver on Sheffield Plate is considerably thicker than that deposited by electro-plating, it will wear with constant cleaning and if this has been excessive, the base metal will show through in the form of a copper tint. Whether we should add such a piece to our collection is entirely a personal matter.

Worn patches on Sheffield Plate have been renovated by replating, this could have taken place during Victorian times or even later. It will be difficult for the new collector to detect such renovations, but as guide, Sheffield Plate has a feint bluish tint, whilst electro-plated silver is whitish. The fused silver of Sheffield Plate is invariably harder than the silver electro-deposited which is more porous and consequently softer.

For the collector interested in Sheffield Plate, the following list has been provided, and we trust that he will find something to his taste and purse from the extensive range of possibilities.

Toast racks, Candelabrum, Candlesticks, Cheese-toasters, Cake baskets, Fruit baskets, Tea pots, Coffee pots, Trays, Jugs, Kettles, Wine coolers, Covered dishes, Coasters, Egg stands, Egg servers, Sugar basins, Tankards, Beakers, Snuffers, Inkstands, spoons and forks, Fish servers, Saucepans, and so on.

SILVER

Silver and gold are probably the two oldest metals known to mankind, their discovery reaching back into the dark ages before recorded history. Old civilizations of the Greek, Romans, Assyrians, and Egyptians were adorning themselves and their dwellings with beautifully decorated silver. Such is its appeal that even simple, plain surfaces of silver have a lustre and feel that delights the senses of most of us, and especially the silver collector.

Pure silver is very soft, and would not be suitable for utilitarian objects or for working if used in its pure state. Therefore it was alloyed with copper in the proportion of 18 dwts copper to 11 ozs, 2 dwts, silver, which produced

London Hallmark for 1810.
(*Assay Office, Goldsmith Hall*)

London Hallmark for 1705.
(*Assay Office, Goldsmith Hall*)

sterling silver, the high quality material from which silverware and plate was made.

Collecting silver can be a very expensive pastime if only the large, fine quality pieces are sought, but if we drop our sights a little, however, and concentrate on the smaller items, we will not find ourselves excluded from the field. Neither will we be forced to accept articles of inferior quality; in fact, it can make the hunt more exciting if our resources are limited. Before we rush out and buy our first piece of silver, it will be as well to learn a little about the subject.

Hallmarks

The introduction of hallmarks was to guarantee the quality, or standard, of the silver used in the manufacture of a particular article. With English silver we can say that the practice started in 1300, during the reign of Edward I, when the first statute of any importance was decreed. This statute stated that all silver had to be assayed and stamped with the head of a leopard before it was offered for sale. A subsequent law of 1363, specified that the maker add his mark. There were various other statutes made during the next 100 years to strengthen the system and in 1477 yet another statute insisted that the Goldsmiths' Company of London ensured that the standard was maintained. Approximately one year later the date letter was introduced and from then hence, the system can be considered to have been established.

English, Scottish and Irish silver is usually hallmarked with characters and symbols that greatly aid the collector. As a guide these are important, but remember it is possible to find good pieces without any marks.

There are normally four or five marks. One mark will show the maker's initials, another is the standard or quality mark which for sterling silver is the " Lion Passant ". (In heraldic terms this means lion walking, or passing, and the lion is shown with head facing and foreleg raised.) Next comes the date letter, this is a letter on a shield, the style of letter and shape of the shield positively identifies the year of hallmarking, which is usually, of course, the year of manufacture.

We can identify the particular assay office where the article was tested and hallmarked from another mark—an anchor for Birmingham, a leopard's head for London, a harp for Dublin, a crown for Sheffield, a castle for Edinburgh and so on.

Silver fish knife with ivory handle. 1799. (Georgian.)
(*Aldate Ltd.*)

Between 1697 and 1720 a higher standard of silver known as " Britannia standard " was compulsory. The lion passant was replaced by a figure of Britannia and the leopard's head by a lion's head erased (torn off the shoulder). The sterling standard was restored in 1720 but the Britannia standard with its special marks continued as an optional second standard.

An additional mark, the reigning sovereign's head, was used between 1784 and 1890 to show that the duty had been paid. The duty on silver was abolished in 1890.

Now where do we start our collection? Do we start with tableware, and use it in the home in a practical way? Good usable domestic silver will not be too expensive, providing we select carefully. It is worth remembering that since the Restoration almost every type of tableware has been produced in silver. Excluding the obvious knives, forks and spoons which are more useful if collected in sets, there are beautiful single pieces of flatware such as cheese-scoops, strainer spoons, apple corers and marrow scoops. Some of the smaller items of holloware such as beakers and tankards will be a little more expensive, but they can be pressed into use.

Ideal pieces for the silver cabinet are snuffboxes, patch-boxes and vinaigrettes. A vinaigrette is a small box, usually beautifully decorated, which has a small grill or grid, to contain a sponge in the base of the box. The sponge was soaked in aromatic vinegar. It was used for inhaling the fumes, which overcame any prevailing bad smells. Vinaigrettes are also known as sponge-boxes, and were produced in other materials than silver, as you will see under the various headings in this book.

Vinaigrettes date from the times of George III (1760–1820) and were in use up to Victorian times. It is interesting to note that the orange carried by Cardinal Wolsey was, in fact, an orange hollowed out, and a sponge substituted to carry the vinegar, as a protection against the plague and other pestilences.

Collecting vinaigrettes will prove a good introduction to silver, the vast majority are marked, and some experience of the field can be gained with little chance of " being caught ". They are usually rectangular, but other shapes are not uncommon. The exteriors are usually beautifully hand engraved, and some of the more desirable types have a raised pattern on the lid.

In the same class as vinaigrettes, and an ideal series to combine in a collection, are patch-boxes, used for carrying court plasters, and spice-boxes, for holding nutmeg, which was grated and sprinkled into wine. These small boxes were produced both in England and on the Con-

Silver Cigarette Case, with figure of golfer in relief. 1907.
(Loco Antiques)

tinent; however, the English type are preferable, they tend to be more robust than the continental variety.

A teapot in Georgian silver makes tea time more pleasurable. I am certain the tea tastes better, and one can appreciate the pot whilst drinking it. With time, perhaps the collector will wish to add a jug for the milk, a basin for sugar and even a tray to put them on. If you advance a collection in this way be certain to obtain the additional pieces in the same style, and date, so that each piece matches, and forms a complete set, rather than add unrelated pieces. A matching set will be more valuable should you wish to re-sell and remember that such a set is likely to be more valuable than the sum of the prices you paid for each individual item.

Whilst on the subject of tableware, salt cellars, mustard pots and the like are relatively cheap. Eighteenth century salt cellars were like a shallow bowl with a moulded base, later ones had three or four feet on which to stand. From about 1765 the shape became oval and the sides pierced, they contained a glass liner for the salt. Early 19th century salt cellars were sometimes designed as miniature tureens. Mustard, until about the middle of the 18th century, was not premixed in a pot. It was presented at table as a powder, in castors with unpierced lids. The user had to mix his own mustard on the side of his plate.

After about 1760, when mustard was premixed, the pots, either cylindrical, or pierced, often contained glass liners and were usually blue in colour. These fairly plain types were followed by oval, and later by the more elegant spherical types.

The field of silver is vast. Any attempt at detailed descriptions of all the possibilities is beyond the scope of any single book.

The following glossary contains short descriptions of generic types. This, it is hoped, will demonstrate the scope to the novice collector, and aid his armchair thinking on the subject.

GLOSSARY

Acanthus: Foliage design originally used on the capitals of Corinthian capitals. The design was used between 16th and 17th centuries for silver, mainly as an embossing.

Almsdish: A circular dish with a flat rim, used for collecting alms.

Annealing: When silver is worked, i.e. formed and hammered, the metal becomes hard and brittle. To restore the metal to a more ductile state, it is carefully heated, or annealed.

Applied: Added to: various parts of silverware are made as separate details, and subsequently joined by the application of solder.

Arabesque: Patterns of flowers and foliage interlaced.

Argyle: A gravy container with a liner for carrying hot water to keep the contents hot. Container usually spouted. First appeared about 1770 and in general use until the early 1800's.

Assay: Test for quality. Metal was removed from the specimen for assay purposes with a scraper.

Baroque: Refers to the late Renaissance period, when decoration became flamboyant with scrolls and natural motifs.

Baskets: Baskets were made to contain fruit, bread, cake and sweetmeats. Early baskets are rare. From about 1730 the basket shape was oval, and had swing handles. Wirework baskets with applied decorations made their appearance about 1770. From about 1800 the shape became circular, like the very early baskets.

Bat's Wing Fluting: A pattern used on hollow-ware resembling the outline of a bat's wing, produced by graduated gadrooning —straight or radiating lines with a raised lobe between the lines.

Beading: Like a bead. Ornamental bordering composed of half spheres, resembling a string of beads.

Beakers: Drinking vessels without handles or stems.

Bells: Table bells of silver, made their first appearance in the 16th century, but English bells are rare prior to the 18th century.

Bezel: An added inside rim.

Biggin: A type of coffee pot, usually with a short spout, often used with a stand and spirit lamp.

Bleeding Bowl: A bowl used by surgeons to catch the blood when blood letting.

Bottle Ticket: Small silver plaques hung on bottles, inscribed to indicate contents. (See Wine and Spirit Labels.)

Brandy Bowls: Mainly of Scandinavian origin, these bowls were used for serving hot brandy during the 17th century. They were flat, with two handles.

Brazier: Bowl with pierced base for burning charcoal, used for heating kettles, etc., during late 17th and early 18th century. Superseded by the spirit lamp and stand.

Buckles: Used for shoes, waistbands, and knee straps, now comparatively rare.

Candelabrum: A candlestick to hold more than one candle. English candelabrum before the 18th century are practically non-existent.

Candlestick: There are many styles and designs of candlesticks, either as single pieces, in pairs, or in sets of four, cast, or made from sheet. 17th century domestic candlesticks are usually square, with a square base.

Canister: A box or container for storing tea.

Cann: A type of mug having rounded sides, standing on a moulded base.

Canteen: A portable case for carrying a knife, fork, spoon, beaker, and condiments. Used by travellers during late 17th and 18th century.

Casters: Containers for pepper, sugar, and mustard. Mustard casters usually had an unpierced lid. Pepper and sugar lids, or covers, were pierced in decorative designs. During the late 18th century, caster bodies changed to glass, and only the tops were made in silver.
17th century style was mainly cylindrical, followed by vase and pear shapes during 18th century.

Censer: An incense burner, now quite rare.

Centre Piece: A decorative piece, often very elaborate in design, used in the centre of a table.

Chalice: A cup, used by the Church for consecrating wine.

Chandelier: Hanging branched candle holders.

Charger: A large decorated dish, intended more for exhibition than for utilitarian purposes.

Cheese-Scoop: First introduced in the late 18th century, cheese-scoops had a curved blade with a silver shaft. Handles were made of ivory, silver, or wood.

Chocolate-Pot: Very similar to a coffee pot, but is fitted with a sliding cover finial which exposes a hole to admit a stirring rod.

Coffee-Pot: Early English examples had either straight or tapering bodies, later examples

polygonal. Pear shaped and classical forms appeared from about 1730.

Compostiera: Container for stewed fruits. Usually two silver jars with glass linings, on a salver-like base.

Cow Cream Jug: A jug in the shape of a cow with lid in the back. Milk pours from the mouth. Introduced into England from Holland about 1755.

Cream Jug: Early examples were pitcher-shaped. Pear shaped bodies supported by three feet were introduced about 1750. Flat bottomed jugs without feet appeared from about 1800. After 1800 the cream jug tended to be part of a tea set and matched the other vessels.

" C "-Scroll: Describes the shape of a handle which resembles a letter " C ".

Cupping Bowl: A bleeding bowl.

Cups: Between the 16th and 17th century a vast number of cups for various uses were made, a few examples follow:—

Candle Cup: Two handled cup for serving candle, and other drinks.

Communion Cup: Equivalent of chalice.

Feeding Cup: Cup with spout for feeding invalids.

Tumbler Cup: Drinking vessel with straight sides and rounded base.

Dram Cup: A shallow bowl, small, with two handles.

Dredger: A kitchen pepper pot with side handle.

Epergne: A table piece containing various dishes for pickles, fruit, etc., usually very elaborate.

Étui: A small case used by ladies to carry bodkin, snuff spoon, etc.

Ewer: Water jugs of elaborate design. Used at meal-times for washing hands in the 16th century.

Finial: Ornamental top to a cover.

Fish-Slice: First introduced about 1750. The slices were made with ivory and wooden handles in addition to silver. Early examples are the most attractive with their pierced and engraved patterns.

Flagon: Container for wine, not unlike large tankards. Not many produced after 1750.

Gadroon: A style of decoration, produced by casting or hammering, used on borders of candlestick bases and the like. The pattern is formed of straight or radiating lines with a raised lobe between the lines.

Goblet: A heavy based, bulbous drinking vessel.

Handles-Bail: A half circle, or half loop hinged handle, similar to the handle on a modern bucket.

Inkstand: 18th century inkstands were mainly a tray with inkpot, pouncebox, taper stick and bell, in one form or another. Earlier examples are rare.

Jewel Boxes: Usually rectangular with hinged lids, some decorated by engraving, but majority moulded or chased.

Jewellery: Broaches, bracelets, buttons, etc., often set with stones.

Ladle: There are various types of ladles, made for specific purposes. Basic shape of a sauce ladle had a deep bowl and a curved handle. Punch ladles had long handles, bowls with double lips date from about 1725. From the 18th century handles were usually horn or whalebone. Earlier examples had long tapering handles of silver.
Cream ladles were smaller versions of sauce ladles.
Soup ladles were also similar to sauce ladles, but with a long stem.
From the latter part of the 18th century, ladle designs, except perhaps those for punch, were made to conform with tea and table sets.

Lemon-Squeezer: A device for squeezing lemons dating from early 19th century, consisting of hinged levers with depression for holding the lemons.

Matting: A matt surface produced by repeated punching with a burred tool.

Mazarine: A flat straining plate used for draining fish dishes.

Meat-Dish: These are found in sizes between about 10 and 30 inches. Usually oval in shape with gadrooned rims after about 1730. From about 1775 beaded rims appear. Early meat dishes have moulded rims.

Moulding: Castings produced from a mould, or border decoration produced by casting or hammering.

Ovolo: A moulding used in the 16th century for border decoration shaped like a small oval. Also used in 18th and early 19th century.

Pannikin: A small drinking cup.

Perfume Burner: These were made in England until about the middle of the 19th century. Late 17th century burners were more elaborate, and they are now rare.

Pin Cushion: Pin cushions with a silver frame may be found from the late 17th century, up to the middle of the 19th century.

Pipkin: A small saucepan-like vessel used to warm brandy. Usually spouted, handle of wood.

Planish: To flatten. Usually executed with an oval faced punch.

Pomander: Box for carrying spices which were used to ward off pestilences, used much the same as vinaigrettes, but often more elaborate in design.

Porringer: A bowl, with or without a lid, having two handles and used for porridge or meats.

Pounce Box: Bottle for holding pounce or sand for sprinkling onto writing.

Pricking: A form of engraving using a needle point to " prick out " the design.

Punch Bowl: Used from the 17th century, to serve punch. The bowl was circular and often had two drop handles.

Quaich: A drinking cup with two or more handles, originated in Scotland.

Raising: A term used to describe the method of " raising " silver plate from a flat sheet into a cup shape. This was done by successive hammerings over wooden blocks to stretch and form the sheet. This operation caused the silver to harden. (See Annealing.)

Reeding: A border moulding of parallel convex convolutions.

Reed and Tie: Similar to reeding, but with cross straps added.

Repoussé Work: A form of relief work obtained by hammering from the under or inner surface, often enhanced by chasing the outline.

Salt-Cellar: 18th century salt-cellars were simply a circular bowl, either with a moulded base or on three or four feet. More elaborate oval shapes with pierced sides and glass liners appeared from about 1765. A few years later the plain boat shape was introduced.

Salver: A flat plate or tray for carrying other vessels. Shapes include circular, oval, rectangular and polygonal, with decorative borders and chasing. Often found raised on tiny feet.

Saucepan: Found from early 18th to early 19th century. Basically a cylindrical or bellied body, sometimes lipped, with wooden handles.

Scent Bottle: Those for carrying on one's person were small, and often pear shaped, and decorated.
Dressing table scent bottles of the 17th century were larger.

Sconce: A wall light. Consisting of a decorated plaque, from which one or more branched candleholders are mounted.

Silver Gilt: Silver over which has been applied a thin coating of gold.

Skewer: Dates from early 18th century. Meat skewers either had a ring, or decorated fan termination to facilitate handling.

Skillet: Saucepan for heating liquids, with legs. Often with covers. Dates from 17th century.

Snuff Box: Found in great varieties from solid silver and with combinations of gem stones, wood, tortoise shell and many other materials.

Snuffers: An instrument for trimming candlewick, similar to a pair of scissors.

Spinning: A method of producing small hollow-ware from sheet by spinning the material on a lathe and forming with hand held, polished surfaced tools.

Spoons: These exist in tremendous varieties, the best known is probably the Apostle spoon with its figures of an apostle full length along the finial.
Spoons were also made for many special purposes, including spoons for Basting, Tea measuring, Dessert, Egg, Marrow, Mustard, Salt, Snuff, Straining, Table, and so on.

Sucket Fork: An instrument with two pronged fork at one end and a spoon at the other, used for eating sweetmeats.

Sugar Bowl: Early 18th century bowls were plain circular, or many sided. Later examples were combined to form matching sets.

Sugar Sifter: A ladle shaped spoon with pierced bowl for sprinkling sugar over food.

Table Services: Complete table services date from the 18th century, where they appeared on the tables of the very wealthy.

Tankard: A beer-drinking vessel, with or without a lid, and a single handle.

Taper Box: Cylindrical box for containing coiled sealing wax taper, dates from about 1700.

Tea Kettle: Designs not unlike teapots, early examples have stands for spirit lamp or charcoal heaters, and late 18th century examples may have a tap replacing the spout. The tea urn made its appearance about 1760.

Tea Pots: English tea pots are found with spherical pear shaped, oval and semi-rectangular bodies. Squat circular shapes were introduced in the early 19th century, together with sugar basin and cream jug, to form a set.

Tea pots can be found from practically the whole of the world.

Toast Rack: These date from about 1770.

Waxjack: Consists of an open frame through which a spindle is fitted to carry coiled sealing taper. One end of the taper is fed through a ring at the top of the frame. Dates from about late 17th century.

TOYS AND GAMES

Toys and games, in one form or another, have been made and used by men and children from very early times. Dolls made of terra-cotta, with movable arms and legs, were certainly used by the Greeks, and there is evidence, provided by excavations, of dolls in the days of ancient Babylon. Unfortunately very few examples of very early toys have survived the passage of time.

Dolls were being made at Nuremburg at least from the 15th century, mainly by wood carvers, and it is probable that they were being made there even earlier. Nuremburg was still an important toy manufacturing centre during Victoria's reign. Collectors usually concentrate on 19th century examples, when mass produced toys of great variety were made to supply the increasing demand. Mechanical toys, powered by clockwork, and almost entirely of German or Swiss origin, were made with great ingenuity, and good quality examples can command high prices.

Like all antiques, good examples are difficult to find at reasonable prices, and toys and games are no exception, but diligent searching will often result in an unexpected find.

Arks

Model arks, with their numerous animals, were originally intended to amuse children on Sundays. It was a quiet pastime, which had the correct religious associations.

It is difficult to say, with any certainty, when model arks were first used, but they were certainly a firm, favourite plaything during the 19th century, and they were manufactured in great numbers from about 1840.

Good quality arks must have been expensive, even during those days, they were generally constructed of wood, with a deep hull that provided storage for the animals and Noah's family, when not in use. The animals were well made, and like the ark, painted in appropriate colours and markings.

Cheaper and simpler arks were made without the deep hull, a single wooden raft served the purpose. The animals, mass produced, were made of wood and plaster, and sometimes quite crudely finished.

As mentioned in the text covering " Bone Carving ", French prisoners of war, captured during the Napoleonic wars, applied themselves to many trades, and the making of model arks was one of their activities.

A beautiful example of prisoner of war work can be seen at the Bethnal Green Museum, it is made of wood and coloured straw, with a deep hull and inset door, the

Noah's Ark of straw-work and wood.
(*Victoria & Albert Museum, Crown copyright*)

"House" has a porch style door and windows. The animals, although somewhat crude, are recognisable.

These early arks were often unpainted, as they were made either of pine with decorative veneer, or were finished with straw-work or marquetry.

Dolls Houses

Dolls houses, known in England from the early 18th century, were originally a German innovation. Initially they were a toy, designed for adults rather than for

Doll's house made under the direction of Queen Mary. English. Made 1887.

(*Victoria & Albert Museum, Crown copyright*)

190

"Caroline" cottage showing interior furnishings. 1831.
(*Victoria & Albert Museum, Crown copyright*)

children and were used as demonstration models for teaching girls the intricacies of running a house. As may be expected, these were only to be seen in the houses of the well-to-do, but during the reign of Victoria, they ceased to be the prerogative of the rich, and almost every Victorian child could then boast of a dolls house of their own.

A typical, good quality dolls house of the late Victorian period would resemble a real house of the period, completely furnished with miniature furniture and utensils. (See the Miles House at Bethnal Green Museum.)

Many of the tiny ornaments, tea-sets, furnishing pieces etc., were made on semi-production lines by skilled craftsmen specifically for dolls houses, and these can form an interesting collection, even if they are not displayed in a dolls house.

Mechanical toy (U.S.A.).   Musical toy (German).
(*Victoria & Albert Museum, Crown copyright*)

Mechanical Toys

These are now in very great demand, especially if they are in good condition and rare. Recent sale prices for such examples exceed £1,000. However, even if the price is above your means it will be interesting to know a little about them.

One such model is an automatous snake charmer, it is almost too exotic to be labelled " Toy ", with a beautifully proportioned standing figure of a girl holding a trumpet in one hand, and a snake in the other hand. The figure stands on a plinth which houses the clockwork. When wound up, music plays, her head moves, her breasts rise and fall, the snake wriggles and she raises the trumpet to her lips. What a toy!

Figures of minstrels and musicians which play a tune from a hidden music box, open their mouths, move their heads, and strum on a musical instrument, are more often

Horse and Hull coach.
(*Victoria & Albert Museum, Crown copyright*)

than not Austrian, and can usually be found at a price much less than the snake charmer.

Clockwork rowing boats, clowns that tumble, trees with birds flying around and singing, are just a few of the possibilities the 19th century offered in mechanical toys.

Horses and Waggons

These were usually a carved horse mounted on a wheeled platform, and propelled by pulling on a length of string, attached to the platform. Sometimes two horses were mounted on a single platform.

Horse and coal cart.
(*Victoria & Albert Museum, Crown copyright*)

1. Doll with face painted wax, dressed to represent a pedlar woman, English. First half 19th century. 13½″ high.

2. Doll with head, hands and feet of painted wax, wearing dress of silk brocade and silver lace, English, but some materials of a later date.

3. Doll with shoulders, head and hands of painted wax, dressed to represent a lady about 1770–80. English about 1770-1780.

(Victoria & Albert Museum, Crown copyright)

Carts were attached to the horse, which was between the shafts, by leather thongs or small chains.

The variety of carts, carriages and coaches are numerous and many are finely executed.

Dolls

Old dolls are collected by a considerable number of people, and they have been doing so for a number of years. Some antique shops even specialise in the subject, so it will not be an easy field to enter.

Pedlar Dolls   Dutch Dolls

Top plate: Doll in costume of 1860–70, English.   Doll in costume of 1830, English.
Doll in costume of Reign of George IV, English.
(*Victoria & Albert Museum, Crown copyright*)

Early European dolls had large heads and faces, and hands made of wood. The eyes were applied in paint. " Queen Anne Dolls " are similar, but they usually have glass eyes and peg-mounted limbs. Dolls made of wood made originally by peasants of the Thuringian Forest, were known in England as " Dutch Dolls ", these dolls had painted hair.

Wax dolls with either wooden, kid or stuffed cloth bodies were made as early as the mid 18th century, but they are generally considered to be a Victorian innovation. Hair was added to some of the wax dolls, strand by strand, using a new technique which employed a hot needle. France gave us the Bisque head and limbs, which were followed by porcelain.

Wax doll about 1845.

Wooden Doll. 1832.

(Victoria & Albert Museum, Crown copyright)

The " Pedlar " dolls were a firm Victorian favourite, so named because they, in fact, " peddled their wares " from little baskets or trays.

The latest development was, of course, the " Sleeping Doll " which closed her eyes when laid flat.

Rocking Horses

Rocking horses of carved wood, mounted on curved rockers, and suitably painted were a common nursery toy. Many examples of these strong, robust, horses have

Cup and ball.

(*Victoria & Albert Museum, Crown copyright*)

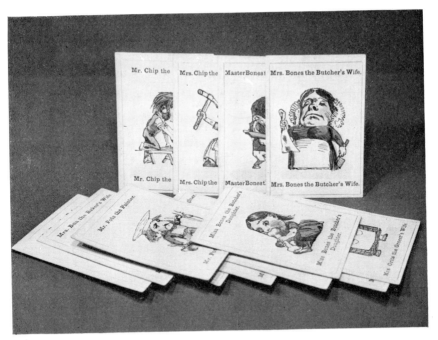

Set of Victorian "Happy Families" playing cards, produced from engravings and coloured by hand.
(*D. C. Gohm*)

survived from the early 19th century when they were in vogue. About 1900 the safety rocking horse was made to prevent accidents caused by over enthusiastic children who over rocked, and so came tumbling off. This type of horse was mounted on a strong fixed frame by " U " shaped links, which permitted a realistic motion although the base was stationary.

Card Games

Card games with an educational bias have always been popular, and they have been produced over the past 100 years or so, in considerable numbers. Victorian children were rarely allowed to play games using normal playing cards, these were considered to be the " devil's cards ".

Specialist collectors are always searching for good quality card games, and they are slowly becoming more

Victorian counter used for scoring in card games.
(*D. C. Gohm*)

difficult to find, except perhaps in museums devoted to toys and the few antique specialists.

"Happy Families" and "Snap" have long been in vogue, but here are a few of the lesser known.

"Panko", this was a Suffragette game in vogue about 1912.

"Geography of England and Wales", which includes the use of a map, dates about 1799.

"Old Maid", dates about 1900.

"Peter Puzzlewigs Mirthful Game of Alliteration", dates about 1840.

"The Wandering Jew", a German set of cards dated about 1832.

"Historical Lotto", a German set of cards dating about 1890.

The majority of the above card games can be seen in the Derby museum and Art Gallery at Wardwick in Derby.

WINE AND SPIRIT LABELS

Collecting wine and spirit labels is a field where there is a reasonable scope and opportunity, and is one that has not been exhaustively collected in the past, therefore the prices of such labels should be reasonable and it should not be too difficult running them to earth.

Such a collection in itself will not necessarily be sufficiently rewarding for anybody who has the collective instinct, but if associated with another collection such as decanters and sealed bottles they could provide a sympathetic adjunct. The majority of wine labels are made of silver, they can be curved in shape to fit the bottle, oval, or rectangular and they can be engraved, pierced, or embossed with a name of a wine, which is surrounded with a beaded, or gadrooned border (gadrooned means a border ornament hammered, or cast with radiating lobes of curved or straight form). The labels usually have two pierced holes, one each end, to which a narrow chain or wire is threaded so that the label can hang from the neck of a bottle or decanter to denote the contents.

Although silver wine labels are only minor items of silver, they were produced by some of the great English silversmiths of the 17th century, and will often carry the maker's mark on the back. Some pieces will be found unmarked but this does not mean that they are not genuine.

Sheffield plate was also used for the manufacture of wine labels, but these are not so easy to find.

Wine labels made of Battersea enamels are probably the most sought after because they were only produced for a very short time between 1753 and 1756. Battersea enamels were made up from thin copper sheet which was covered with a vitreous material to which oxide and tin had been added to make it opaque. After firing this resembled Delftware. The surface was then painted with metallic pigments and the colours fixed by kilning at a low temperature. The Battersea factory was started by

G[1]

Alderman Steven Theodore Janssen, just prior to 1753. However, he became bankrupt in 1756 and his products were sold off, these included many items that could be considered trinkets, things like sleeve buttons, crosses, toothpick cases and of course bottle tickets " with chains for all sorts of liquor and of different subjects ".

There were not many painted enamels from Battersea, most of these were transfer printed. The discovery of transfer printing for Battersea has been attributed to Simon-Francois Ravenet, an engraver of note, who incidentally engraved the plates for Hogarth's Marriage a la Mode.

Wine labels are also to be found in porcelain, mother-of-pearl, and a few other materials. The mother-of-pearl labels are quite uncommon. Many of the names on wine labels are self explanatory, but a few will crop up that are not so common, for instance " Shrub " is a cordial made of fruit juice and spirit. " Cream of the Valley ", this was simply another name for Gin. " Nig " was, in fact, Gin spelt backwards to deceive servants. " Mountain ", a wine from Malaga. " Paraketta ", this denoted an Andalusian wine. " Montrachet ", a wine from a district of that name. " Morachee ", probably a corruption of Montrachet.

The best way to collect wine labels and spirit labels would be to generalise. If you confine them to silver they will certainly offer the larger field, but the collection can be made far more interesting if you include the enamels and porcelains; these are, of course, more difficult to find and it is unlikely that you will be able to form a large collection of these choice items only.

GENERAL INFORMATION
GENERAL PERIODS
ENGLISH

Tudor	1485 to 1558	Reigns of Henry VII
		Henry VIII
		Edward VI
		Mary
Elizabethan	1558 to 1603	Reign of Elizabeth
Jacobean	1603 to 1649	Reigns of James I
		Charles I
Commonwealth	1649 to 1660	Cromwell
Late Stuart	1660 to 1689	Reigns of Charles II
		James II
William & Mary	1689 to 1702	Reign of William & Mary
Queen Anne	1702 to 1727	Reigns of Anne
		George I
Georgian	1727 to 1820	Reigns of George II
		George III
*Regency	1800 to 1830	Reigns of George III
		Prince George
Victorian	1830 to 1901	Reign of Victoria

* Note.—The Regency period should only cover the period when Prince George acted as Regent between 1811 and 1820, but the periods shown are accepted for period classification of antiques generally.

FRENCH

Francois-Premier	1515 to 1547	Reign of Francis I
Henri-Deux	1547 to 1559	,, ,, Henry II
	1559 to 1560	,, ,, Francis II
	1560 to 1574	,, ,, Charles IX
	1574 to 1589	,, ,, Henry III
Henri-Quatre	1589 to 1610	,, ,, Henry IV
Louis-Treize	1610 to 1643	,, ,, Louis XIII
Louis-Quatorze	1643 to 1715	,, ,, Louis XIV
Louis-Quinze	1715 to 1774	,, ,, Louis XV
Louis-Seize	1774 to 1793	,, ,, Louis XVI
Empire	1799 to 1814	Napoleon

DATES OF REIGNING KINGS & QUEENS OF ENGLAND

Period	Sovereign
1066–1087	William I
1087–1100	William II
1100–1135	Henry I
1135–1154	Stephen
1154–1189	Henry II
1189–1199	Richard I
1199–1216	John
1216–1272	Henry III
1272–1307	Edward I
1307–1327	Edward II
1327–1377	Edward III
1377–1399	Richard II
1399–1413	Henry IV
1413–1422	Henry V
1422–1461	Henry VI
1461–1470	Edward IV (1st reign)
1470–1471	Henry VI (restored)
1471–1483	Edward IV (2nd reign)
1483	Edward V
1483–1485	Richard III
1485–1509	Henry VII
1509–1547	Henry VIII
1547–1553	Edward VI
1553–1554	Mary
1554–1558	Phillip & Mary
1558–1603	Elizabeth I
1603–1625	James I
1625–1649	Charles I
1649–1660	Commonwealth
1660–1685	Charles II
1685–1688	James II
1688–1694	William & Mary
1694–1702	William III
1702–1714	Anne
1714–1727	George I
1727–1760	George II

Period	Sovereign
1760–1820	George III
1820–1830	George IV
1830–1837	William IV
1837–1901	Victoria
1901–1910	Edward VII
1910–1936	George V
1936–1952	George VI
1952–	Elizabeth II

DATES OF REIGNING KINGS OF FRANCE

Period	Sovereign
1515–1547	Francis I
1547–1559	Henry II
1559–1560	Francis II
1560–1574	Charles IX
1574–1589	Henry III
1589–1610	Henry IV
1610–1643	Louis XIII
1643–1715	Louis XIV
1715–1774	Louis XV
1774–1793	Louis XVI
1799–1814	Napoleon

REGISTRY MARKS

Porcelain, glass, and many other objects can be dated by analysis of the Registry Mark. This mark was introduced by the British Patent Office, and was in use from 1842 to 1883 incl.

The mark is a vertical diamond, capped with a near full sphere, with semi-circles under each point of the diamond. (See illustrations.)

The hemisphere was reserved for the class of goods, i.e. a. Roman IV, indicated " Glass and Ceramics ". The four points of the diamonds indicate year, month and date manufactured, and the parcel number. In the year 1868, the mark was slightly modified with respect to the positions indicating date of manufacture, but the overall shape remained the same.

Index letters from 1842 to 1867:

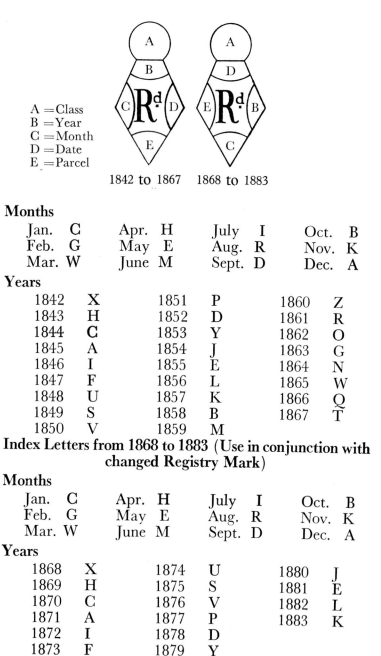

A = Class
B = Year
C = Month
D = Date
E = Parcel

1842 to 1867   1868 to 1883

Months

Jan.	C	Apr.	H	July	I	Oct.	B
Feb.	G	May	E	Aug.	R	Nov.	K
Mar.	W	June	M	Sept.	D	Dec.	A

Years

1842	X	1851	P	1860	Z
1843	H	1852	D	1861	R
1844	C	1853	Y	1862	O
1845	A	1854	J	1863	G
1846	I	1855	E	1864	N
1847	F	1856	L	1865	W
1848	U	1857	K	1866	Q
1849	S	1858	B	1867	T
1850	V	1859	M		

Index Letters from 1868 to 1883 (Use in conjunction with changed Registry Mark)

Months

Jan.	C	Apr.	H	July	I	Oct.	B
Feb.	G	May	E	Aug.	R	Nov.	K
Mar.	W	June	M	Sept.	D	Dec.	A

Years

1868	X	1874	U	1880	J
1869	H	1875	S	1881	E
1870	C	1876	V	1882	L
1871	A	1877	P	1883	K
1872	I	1878	D		
1873	F	1879	Y		

Classes

I	Designs in metal.
II	Designs in wood.
III	Designs in glass.
IV	Designs in earthenware, porcelain, ivory, bone.
V	Designs in paperhanging.
VI	Designs in carpets, floor, or oil cloths.
VII	Designs in shawls, printed patterns.
VIII	Designs in shawls, patterns not printed.
IX	Yarn, thread.
X	Woven fabrics, excluding furniture.
XI	Woven fabrics furniture, printed patterns.
XII	Woven fabrics patterns not printed.
XIII	Lace and all other articles.

EXAMPLES OF CHINA MARKS

Spode

This index of marks, although it contains more than the standard reference books supply, cannot pretend to be complete since, in addition to those given, others are known to occur.

The colours given for the various marks are those most frequently seen, other colours were certainly used for the same mark on other pieces.

In the long period of 200 years innumerable marks were used. In addition to pattern numbers, there were also marks to designate size or shape and a variety of makers' marks such as crosses, stars, triangles, etc. Faced with this multitude, it is doubtful if the complete facts will ever be assembled. We have, however, tried to collect the largest number of important marks and arrange them in chronological order.

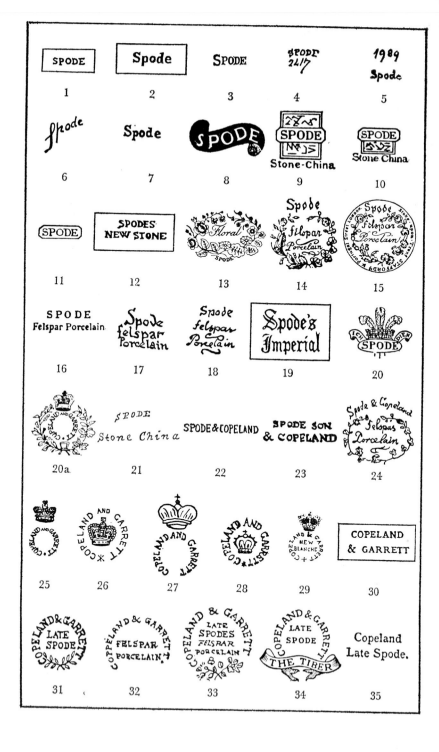

SPODE	Spode	SPODE	SPODE 24/7	1989 Spode
1	2	3	4	5
Spode	Spode	SPODE	SPODE Stone-China	SPODE Stone China
6	7	8	9	10
SPODE	SPODES NEW STONE	Floral SPODE	Spode Felspar Porcelain	Spode Felspar Porcelain
11	12	13	14	15
SPODE Felspar Porcelain	Spode felspar Porcelain	Spode felspar Porcelain	Spode's Imperial	SPODE
16	17	18	19	20
COPELAND AND GARRET	SPODE Stone China	SPODE & COPELAND	SPODE SON & COPELAND	Spode & Copeland Felspar Porcelain
20a.	21	22	23	24
COPELAND AND GARRETT	COPELAND AND GARRETT	COPELAND AND GARRETT	COPELAND AND GARRETT	COPELAND AND GARRETT NEW BLANCHE	COPELAND & GARRETT
25	26	27	28	29	30
COPELAND & GARRETT LATE SPODE	COPELAND & GARRETT FELSPAR PORCELAIN	COPELAND & GARRETT LATE SPODES FELSPAR PORCELAIN	COPELAND & GARRETT LATE SPODE THE TIBER	Copeland Late Spode.
31	32	33	34	35

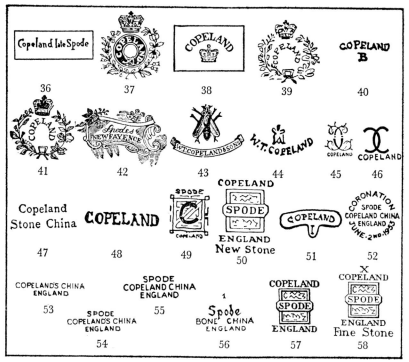

1, 2, impressed, c. 1770; 3, underglaze blue, c. 1784; 4 – 6, red, handpainted, from 1790; 7, 8 underglaze blue, printed c. 1790 – 1805; 9 – 11, underglaze, printed in various colours – blue, brown, black, from 1805; 12, impressed, c. 1805 – 1827; 13 – 16, printed, usually in brown, black or purple; 17 – 18 painted in purple; 19, underglaze blue print, c. 1810; 20 (rare), red print c. 1806; 21 – 24, underglaze blue, printed, c. 1815; 20a, green print, 1833 – 1847; 25 – 29, printed in various colours, usually in green on china and in blue on earthenware 1833 – 1847; 30, impressed; 31 – 34, printed in various colours, 1833 – 1847; 35 – 36, underglaze blue print and impressed, 1847 – 1867; 37 (rare) gold, blue and green print, 1851; 38 – 51, impressed, underglaze blue, green or other colours, from c. 1850 to early twentieth century; 52, gold print, 1953; 53, green print, c. 1862 – 1920; 54, green print, c. 1900 – 1954; 55, green print, 1954 – 1960; 56, green print, 1960; 57, printed on earthenware 1920; 58, printed, 1960.

(Spode marks reproduced by kind permission of W. T. Copeland & Sons Ltd., from their Exhibition Catalogue "Spode Copeland" 1765—1965).

WEDGWOOD MARKS

wedgwood — Assumed to be the first mark, used between 1759 and 1769

WEDGWOOD — A rare mark used at the Bell Pottery

WEDGWOOD / Wedgwood — Used in varying sizes between 1759 and 1769

WEDGWOOD & BENTLEY (circular) — Earliest form of partnership mark

W. & B.
Wedgwood & Bentley: Etruria
Wedgwood & Bentley (circular)
WEDGWOOD & BENTLEY
— In use between 1769 and 1780

Wedgwood / Wedgwood / WEDGWOOD / WEDGWOOD — In use in varying sizes after 1780

WEDGWOOD & SONS — In use for a short period during 1790

JOSIAH WEDGWOOD Feb. 2nd 1805 — Found only on some tripod incense burners

WEDGWOOD — On Bone China, printed in red, blue or gold

Reproduced by kind permission of The Wedgwood Society of London

210

MISCELLANEOUS MARKS.

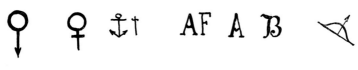

Bow

Bow   Chelsea   Caughley

Caughley   Derby

Minton   Goss

Plymouth   Swansea

Worcester

Rockingham

WINE GLASS BOWL SHAPES.

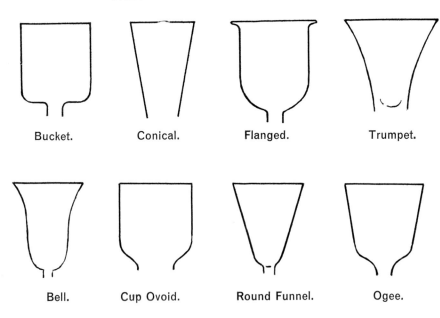

| Bucket. | Conical. | Flanged. | Trumpet. |
| Bell. | Cup Ovoid. | Round Funnel. | Ogee. |

WINE-GLASS KNOPS.

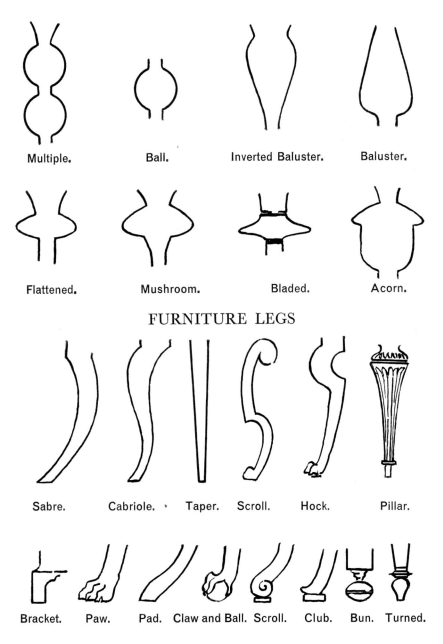

Multiple.	Ball.	Inverted Baluster.	Baluster.

Flattened.	Mushroom.	Bladed.	Acorn.

FURNITURE LEGS

Sabre.	Cabriole.	Taper.	Scroll.	Hock.	Pillar.

Bracket.	Paw.	Pad.	Claw and Ball.	Scroll.	Club.	Bun.	Turned.

HISTORY OF WEDGWOOD

(Reproduced by kind permission of The Wedgwood Society of London)

1730 Birth of Josiah Wedgwood I, and of Thomas Bentley

1739 Death of Thomas Wedgwood, **father of Josiah I**

1740

1745 Birth of Thomas Byerley, **nephew of** Josiah Wedgwood

1750

1760

1762 First meeting with Thomas Bentley

1764 Marriage to cousin,
1740 Sarah Wedgwood

1768 Bentley partnership

1769 Birth of Josiah II (Died 1843)

1769 ETRURIA

(1769 to 1950)

1770

1780 Death of Thomas Bentley

1782 Josiah I elected F.R.S.

1786 Josiah I elected F.S.A.

1788 Death of Thomas Wedgwood partner in making ' useful ' wares

1790 Wedgwood, Sons & Byerley

1795 Death of Josiah Wedgwood I

1800

1810 Death of Thomas Byerley

1820

1744 Apprenticed to eldest brother at the Churchyard Pottery

1749 In partnership with Alders and Harrison at Cliff Bank Pottery

1754 In partnership with Thomas Whieldon at Fenton Low

1759 On own account at Ivy House Pottery

1764 Brick House (later, Bell) Pottery

1740 Agate, black, tortoiseshell, cabbage, cauliflower, salt-glazed and cream wares Experiments to improve bodies and glazes

1761 First employment of Sadler & Green, Liverpool for transfer-printing

1763 Red stoneware, later called 'rosso antico'

1765 Cream ware improved and named ' Queen's Ware '

1766 Basaltes

1770 Cane ware

1774 Jasper ware

1777 ' Jasper Dip '

1780 Pearl ware, and ' **Waxen Jasper** '

1786 Bamboo and Mortar wares

1790 First copy of Portland Vase

1796 Pastry ware 1796 to 1805

1810 Introduction of Smear glaze

1812 Manufacture of Bone China 1812-**16**

1766 Commencement of Grand Trunk Canal

1768 Opening of Newport Street showroom

1769 First employment of William Hackwood

1769 Patent granted for encaustic painting

1769 Painting shop at **Chelsea (**1769-74)

1773 1773 Catalogue

1773 Russian service ordered

1774 Showroom opened in Greek Street

1774 1774 Catalogue

1775 John Flaxman first employed

1775 Richard Champion's petition to Parliament

1775 Reissue of 1774 Catalogue

1777 Grand Trunk Canal completed

1779 1779 Catalogue

1782 Pyrometer described to Royal Society

1786 Portland Vase sold by auction

1787 1787 Catalogue

LONDON DATE LETTERS

from 1716 to 1916

A	1716–7	a	1736–7	A	1756–7	a	1776–7
B	1717–8	b	1737–8	B	1757–8	b	1777–8
C	1718–9	c	1738–9	C	1758–9	c	1778–9
D	1719–20	d	1739–40	D	1759–60	d	1779–80
E	1720–1	e	1740–1	E	1760–1	e	1780–1
F	1721–2	f	1741–2	F	1761–2	f	1781–2
G	1722–3	g	1742–3	G	1762–3	g	1782–3
H	1723–4	h	1743–4	H	1763–4	h	1783–4
I	1724–5	i	1744–5	J	1764–5	i	1784–5
K	1725–6	k	1745–6	K	1765–6	k	1785–6
L	1726–7	l	1746–7	L	1766–7	l	1786–7
M	1727–8	m	1747–8	M	1767–8	m	1787–8
N	1728–9	n	1748–9	N	1768–9	n	1788–9
O	1729–30	o	1749–50	O	1769–70	o	1789–90
P	1730–1	p	1750–1	P	1770–1	p	1790
Q	1731–2	q	1751–2	Q	1771–2	q	1791
R	1732–3	r	1752–3	R	1772–3	r	1792
S	1733–4	ſ	1753–4	S	1773–4	s	1793
T	1734–5	t	1754–5	T	1774–5	t	1794
V	1735–6	u	1755–6	U	1775–6	u	1795–6

215

Ⓐ	1796–7	ⓐ	1816–7	𝕬	1836–7	𝖆	1856–7
Ⓑ	1797–8	ⓑ	1817–8	𝕭	1837–8	𝖇	1857–8
Ⓒ	1798–9	ⓒ	1818–9	𝕮	1838–9	𝖈	1858–9
Ⓓ	1799–00	ⓓ	1819–20	𝕯	1839–40	𝖉	1859–60
Ⓔ	1800–1	ⓔ	1820–1	𝕰	1840–1	𝖊	1860–1
Ⓕ	1801–2	ⓕ	1821–2	𝕱	1841–2	𝖋	1861–2
Ⓖ	1802–3	ⓖ	1822–3	𝕲	1842–3	𝖌	1862–3
Ⓗ	1803–4	ⓗ	1823–4	𝕳	1843–4	𝖍	1863–4
Ⓘ	1804–5	ⓘ	1824–5	𝕴	1844–5	𝖎	1864–5
Ⓚ	1805–6	ⓚ	1825–6	𝕶	1845–6	𝖐	1865–6
Ⓛ	1806–7	ⓛ	1826–7	𝕷	1846–7	𝖑	1866–7
Ⓜ	1807–8	ⓜ	1827–8	𝕸	1847–8	𝖒	1867–8
Ⓝ	1808–9	ⓝ	1828–9	𝕹	1848–9	𝖓	1868–9
Ⓞ	1809–10	ⓞ	1829–30	𝕺	1849–50	𝖔	1869–70
Ⓟ	1810–1	ⓟ	1830–1	𝕻	1850–1	𝖕	1870–1
Ⓠ	1811–2	ⓠ	1831–2	𝕼	1851–2	𝖖	1871–2
Ⓡ	1812–3	ⓡ	1832–3	𝕽	1852–3	𝖗	1872–3
Ⓢ	1813–4	ⓢ	1833–4	𝕾	1853–4	𝖘	1873–4
Ⓣ	1814–5	ⓣ	1834–5	𝕿	1854–5	𝖙	1874–5
Ⓤ	1815–6	ⓤ	1835–6	𝖀	1855–6	𝖚	1875–6

A	1876–7	a	1896–7
B	1877–8	b	1897–8
C	1878–9	c	1898–9
D	1879–80	d	1899–00
E	1880–1	e	1900–1
F	1881–2	f	1901–2
G	1882–3	g	1902–3
H	1883–4	h	1903–4
I	1884–5	i	1904–5
K	1885–6	k	1905–6
L	1886–7	l	1906–7
M	1887–8	m	1907–8
N	1888–9	n	1908–9
O	1889–90	o	1909–10
P	1890–1	p	1910–1
Q	1891–2	q	1911–2
R	1892–3	r	1912–3
S	1893–4	s	1913–4
T	1894–5	t	1914–5
U	1895–6	u	1915–6

Further Reading

The Silk Pictures of Thomas Stevens, by Wilma Sinclair Le Van Baker, published by Exposition Press, New York.

Print Collectors Handbook, by Whitman and Salaman, published by G. Bell and Sons Ltd. London.

Pewter Down the Ages, by Howard Herschel Cotterell, published by Hutchinson and Co. (Publishers) Ltd. London.

Pewter Collecting for Amateurs, by Kenneth Ullyett, published by Frederick Muller Ltd.

English Silver, by Judith Banister, published by Ward, Lock and Co. Ltd.

English Domestic Silver, by Charles Oman, published by Adam and Charles Black.

Handbook of Pottery and Porcelain Marks, by W. B. Honey and J. B. Cushion.

English Glass for the Collector 1660–1860, by G. Bernard Hughes, published by Lutterworth Press.

Pocket Book of Glass, by Geoffrey Wills, published by Country Life Ltd. London.

Josiah Wedgwood and his Pottery, by William Burton, published by Cassell and Co. Ltd.

British Portrait Miniatures, by Daphne Foskett, published by Methuen and Co. Ltd.

British Pottery and Porcelain, by Geoffrey A. Godden, F.R.S.A. published by Herbert Jenkins Ltd.

18th Century English Porcelain, by George Savage, published by Spring Books.

Prisoners-of-War-Work, by Jane Toller, published by the Golden Head Press.

World of Toys, by Leslie Daiken, published by Lambards Press.

A B C for Book Collectors, by John Carter, published by Hart-Davis, London.

English Coins, by G. C. Brooke, published by Methuen, London.

Collecting Coins, by Frank Purvey, published by Foyle, London.

Old English, Irish, and Scottish Table Glass, by G. Bernard Hughes, published by Batsford Press.

Aquatint Engraving, by G. T. Prideaux, published by W. & G. Foyle, London.

... All available from

Foyles of London.

INDEX

INDEX